RESEARCH BIBLIOGRAPHIES & CHECKLISTS

2

André Breton

Supplement N° 1

RESEARCH BIBLIOGRAPHIES & CHECKLISTS

RₑB

General Editors

A.D. Deyermond, J.R. Little and J.E. Varey

ANDRÉ BRETON

a bibliography (1972-1989)

(Supplement to Michael Sheringham:
André Breton, a Bibliography)

ELZA ADAMOWICZ

Grant & Cutler Ltd
1992

© Grant & Cutler Ltd
1992
ISBN 0 7293 0343 8

I.S.B.N. 84-599-3279-6

DEPÓSITO LEGAL: V. 1.004 - 1992

Printed in Spain by Artes Gráficas Soler, S.A., Valencia
for

GRANT & CUTLER LTD
55-57 GREAT MARLBOROUGH STREET, LONDON W1V 2AY

Contents

INTRODUCTION

The aim of this *Supplement* to Michael Sheringham's *André Breton. A Bibliography* (1972) is primarily to continue the record of André Breton's texts and critical and biographical material on Breton. In order to ensure continuity, criteria for the selection and presentation of the entries have on the whole followed those applied in the first volume. Minor changes in presentation are explained below.

The *Supplement* is divided into two sections, Primary Material and Secondary Material.

A. *Primary Material*

The same chronological sequence and order of entries as in the first volume have been retained. Within each year items are identified by the following reference letters according to type of text:

Aa: Books and pamphlets written by Breton, and publications edited by him.

Ab: Articles, poems, reviews, interviews, etc. by Breton published in periodicals.

Ac: Prefaces, introductions, poems and other texts published in books by other authors or in collective volumes.

Ad: Manifestoes, tracts, broadsheets, collective declarations, written and/or signed by Breton in collaboration with others.

As in the first volume, reprints are listed in smaller type at the end of each year, when appropriate.

The primary material is, however, divided into two sub-sections in the present volume :

        (i) Breton's publications before 1972.   These include complementary information on original entries, as well as new entries. Numbering has followed the original chronological order, new entries thus slotting into the original sequence, and identified with an additional letter, for example Ad97a, Ab97b. Where an earlier publication of an item has been recorded, a new item code has been given, with the original item code in brackets after the title, for example: Ab293a 'Visite à Léon Trotsky' [Aa506.1]. A cross-reference to this new entry is given at the original entry number.

(ii) Publication of Breton's texts from 1972 to 1989. Numbering follows on from the first volume, and thus begins at Aa744. Cross-references are given where applicable to entries in both volumes.

Some articles by Breton translated into languages other than English have been included with the Primary material for their socio-political interest, for example the articles published in Spanish in the anarchist publication *Solidaridad obrera* [Ad482b, Ab488a].

At: This section [starting at At946] covers translations of Breton's texts into English.

B. *Secondary Material*

The large number of memoirs, letters and interviews published by Breton's contemporaries in the period covered by this *Supplement* offers abundant information on Breton, much of considerable interest to scholars, some seemingly trivial. Although the aim of the present bibliography is primarily to present a record of critical material on Breton, items of an anecdotal or polemical nature have been included when they shed interesting light on his work or life-history.

The facsimile reprints of major surrealist journals and the recent publication of the first volume of Breton's *Œuvres complètes* in the Pléiade edition have contributed to the availability of Breton's texts. Moreover, the critical application of (post)structuralist theory and the publication of specialised Surrealist periodicals (*Mélusine*, *Pleine marge*) are evidence of renewed interest in Breton in recent years, focusing less on his role within Surrealism, as in earlier years, than on analyses of his texts. There has also been an important development of critical interest in Breton and Surrealism in Italy, Central Europe and South America, which the present *Supplement* has attempted to record without claiming to be exhaustive in these areas.

As in the first volume, an alphabetical sequence has been retained for this section, both for authors and articles. Unlike the first volume, however, this section has been divided into four parts :

Ba. Books and periodicals published between 1972 and 1989, wholly or substantially devoted to Breton. The numbering follows on from the first volume, starting with Ba38.

Bb. This part is divided into two sub-sections:

(i) Articles and less substantial parts of books published before 1972. As in Section A, these include complementary information on original entries, as well as new entries. Numbering has followed an alphabetical order. new entries slotting into the original sequence, and identified with an additional letter, as in Primary Material.

(ii) Articles and less substantial parts of books published between 1972 and 1989. Numbering follows on from the first volume, and therefore begins at Bb804.

Bc. Theses. Only doctorates have been included. These have been listed in a separate section, because of the large number written since Breton's death. Numbering in this section begins at Bc1600.

Presentation follows that of the first volume: volume numbers are indicated in Roman numerals, issue numbers in Arabic numerals. Dates are given in the language of the country of publication. An asterisk after an entry indicates that I have not personally seen the item, having relied on secondary sources for my information.

I have benefited at all stages in the preparation of this bibliography from the advice and criticism of Michael Sheringham to whom I would like to extend my warmest thanks. I should also like to thank the following: Roger Little for his advice and close scrutiny of the manuscript; the staff of the Bibliothèque Nationale de Paris and Goldsmiths' College Library, London; the Champs des Activités Surréalistes at the C.N.R.S. whose bibliographical publication *Signes* I particularly appreciated; François Crompton-Roberts from the Arts Computing Unit, Queen Mary and Westfield College, for the preparation of the camera-ready copy; and Peter Dunwoodie, each time the rigours of *bibliophilie* bordered on the excesses of *bibliofolie*.

Elza ADAMOWICZ
University of London

A : PRIMARY MATERIAL

(i) Publications before 1972

1912

Ab1a.1   'Le Rêve'. See Aa839.
Ab1a.2   'Eden...'. See Aa839.
          Vers l'idéal (Lycée Chaptal) (mai 12). Signed anagrammatically
          René Dobrant.*

1919

Ab16a   Aa15.1 first published in *L'Éventail* (Geneva), II, 2 (15 fév.19).
          See Aa839.

Ab16b   Aa15.2 first published in *Valori plastici* (Rome), I, 2–3
          (febbr.–marzo 19), 15. See Aa839.*

1920

Ab42a   Letter to Rachilde (1 avr.20), *Comœdia*, XIV, 2666 (4 avr.20),
          2. See Aa839.

Ab46   Title to read: 'Les Contes du *Cannibale*'.

1921

Ac56   Date to read: 1921.

Ac61a   Ac56 [quoted in full] in Bb187b. See Aa839.

1922

Ab70a   'Quelques préférences', in Ab70, p.2. See Ab786, Aa839.

Ad82   Journal ref.: *Comœdia*, XVI, 3306 (3 jan.22), 2. See Aa839.

Ad82a   'Résolution du Comité pour le Congrès de Paris', *ibid.*, XVI, 3341 (7 fév.22), 1.

Ad84a   Ad82 in *L'Ere nouvelle*, IV, 735 (3 jan.22), unpag.[3].

Ad84b   Ad82a in *ibid.* (7 fév.22).*

1923

Ab87   Add: Includes Aa85.4.

Ab90   Journal ref.: *Le Journal du peuple*, VIII, 15 (7 avr.23), 3.

Ad97a   'Réponse à l'enquête: Le Symbolisme a-t-il dit son dernier mot?' (18 fév.23), *Le Disque vert*, 4–5–6 (fév.–mars–avr.23), 112. See Ac797.

Ab97b   Aa85.7 in *Le Journal du peuple*, VIII, 44 (1 déc.23), 3.

1924

Ab101a   'Robert Desnos', *Le Journal littéraire*, 11 (5 juil.24), 13. See Aa839.

Ab105a   'La Querelle du surréalisme (mise au point d'AB)', *Comœdia*, 4263 (24 août 24), 2.

Ab105b   Letter to Desnos (11 oct.24), quoted by Picabia in 'Dernière heure', *391*, 19 (oct.24), 3. See Ac631b, 788.

Ab105d   'Recherches surréalistes', *Les Nouvelles littéraires* (8 nov.24), 2. Unsigned, but MS evidence shows text was written by AB. See Ab127c, Ac766, Aa839.

Ad108a   Letter to Directors of *Les Nouvelles littéraires* (26 mai 24), *Le Journal littéraire*, 6 (31 mai 24), 6. See Ac797.

Ad109a   Ad105 in *Les Nouvelles littéraires*, III, 99 (6 sept.24), 1. See Ac709, Ac797, Aa839.

Ad109b   'Encore le surréalisme', *Le Journal littéraire*, 18 (23 août 24), 8. See Ac797.

Ad110a   Letter to Pierre Morhange (11 oct.24), *Le Journal littéraire*, 26 (18 oct.24), 5. See Ac797.

Ab111   Journal ref.: *Paris-journal*, XXXVIII, n.s., 2486 (1 fév.24), 3.

Ab111a   Text 20 from Aa99.2, *Images de Paris*, V, 55 (août 24).

Ab111b   'La Querelle du surréalisme. M. AB répond' [Extract from Aa99], *Le Journal littéraire*, 20 (6 sept.24), 10.

Ad111c   Aa85.12 in *Paris-journal*, XXXV, 2483 (11 jan.24), 3. See Aa839.

Ad111d   Ad110a in *NRF*, XXII, 134 (nov.24), 643. Includes extracts of Morhange's reply. See Ac797.

1925

Ab114a   'Enquête des *Cahiers du mois*: Orient/Occident', *Les Cahiers du mois*, 9–10 (fév.–mars 25), 250–51. See Aa839.

Ad126a   'Appel aux travailleurs intellectuels. Oui ou non, condamnez-vous la guerre?', *L'Humanité*, 7901 (2 juil.25), 1. See Ad127d, Ac794, 797.

Ad126b   'Un appel à l'opinion publique (la répression en Pologne)', *L'Humanité*, 9738 (8 août 25), 2. See Ac797.

Ad126c   'Lettre ouverte aux autorités roumaines', *L'Humanité*, 9758 (28 août 25), 1, 3. See Ac797.

Ad127a   '*Clarté, Philosophies, La Révolution surréaliste* solidaires du Comité Central d'Action. Aux soldats et aux marins', *L'Humanité*, 9807 (16 oct.25), 2. See Ac797.

Ad127b   'Télégramme au Président du Conseil de Hongrie', *L'Humanité*, 9808 (17 oct 25), 3. See Ac797.

Ab127c   Ab105c, under title 'Le Bureau de recherches surréalistes', in *La Révolution surréaliste* [see Ab112], p.31. See Ab766, Aa839.

Ad127d   Ad126a in *Clarté*, 76 (15 juil.25), 285. See Ac794, 797.

Ad127e   Ad127 in *L'Humanité*, 9782 (21 sept.25), 2. See Ad127f, Ac721a, 766, 794, 798.

Ad127f   Ad127 in *Clarté*, 77 (15 oct.25). See Ac721a, 766, 797.*

1927

Ad151a   Ad149 [quoted in full] in *Clarté*, VI, n.s., 11 (15 juil.27), 347–48. See Ac721a, Ac797, Aa839.

1928

Ab159a   'Littérature prolétarienne?' [reply to survey], *Monde*, I, 14 (8 sept.28), 4.

1930

Aa174a   *Second manifeste du surréalisme* [Aa175], Paris: Kra (Club des Soixante), 1930 (20 juin), 104pp. Pre-original edn., 60 copies (50 copies for Corti, numbered I-L; one copy bound in polished nickel for René Gaffé). Frontispiece by Dali. Contains Ab167 as offprint.

Ab176a   Aa195.3, 195.4, 195.5, 195.6, 195.7 (no titles) in *Nemoguce-L'Impossible* [bilingual], Belgrade: Éditions Surréalistes, print. 1930.*

Ac182a   'Prière d'insérer', in René Char, *Artine*, Paris: Éditions Surréalistes, 1930. See Aa839.*

Ad184   Title to read: *La Femme visible*. See Ad194a, Ac721a, Ac797.

1931

Ad190a   'Les Intellectuels français protestent contre la terreur en Chine', *L'Humanité*, 12032 (23 nov.31), 3. See Ac797.

Ad194a   Ad184 in *Les Cahiers d'art*, VI, 1 (1931), 60. See Ac721a, Ac797.

1932

Ad203a   Texts from Ad185 and 191 in brochure published for first screening of *L'Age d'or* in Belgium. See Ac794.*

1933

Ad215a   'Protestez!' [AB among the A.E.A.R. signatories], *Feuille rouge*, 2 (mars 33), 2. See Ac797.

Ad215b   'Les écrivains et artistes révolutionnnaires saluent les grévistes des usines Citroën', *ibid.*, 3 (1 mai 33), 1.

Ad215c   'Contre le fascisme mais aussi contre l'impérialisme français' [AB among the A.E.A.R. signatories], *ibid.*, 4, n.d. [mai–juin 33], 2.

1934

Ac230a   Text 26 from Aa99.2, 186, 195.4, 195.11, 195.19, Ab17, 20, 85.9, 93.4, in Georges Hugnet, *Petite Anthologie poétique du surréalisme*, Paris: Jeanne Bucher, 1934.

Ab245   MS evidence shows that text was written by Éluard alone.

1935

Ab236a   'Saludo a Tenerife', *La Tarde* (9 mayo 35).*

Ab237a   'Posición política del surrealismo' [extracts from lecture given at Athenaum of Santa Cruz], *Gaceta de arte*, 35 (1935).*

Ab237b   'Despedida y recuerdo de Tenerife', *La Tarde* (1 junio 35).*

Ad249   Title to read 'Cycle systématique de conférences...'

1936

Ab257a   [Ed., With Éluard], *Konkretion*, 5–6, sp.no. (mars 36). Includes texts by AB.*

Ad267a   'La Rupture avec *Contre-attaque*', *L'Œuvre* (24 mars 36). See Ac797.*

1937

Ad287a   'En marge de l'exposition du Jeu de Paume. Une lettre ouverte au Président du Conseil', *Beaux-arts*, 242 (20 août 37), 1, 4.

1938

Ab293a   'Visite à Léon Trotsky' [Aa506.1], first published in *Quatrième internationale*, 14–15 (nov.–déc.38), 242–47.
Also contains Ad297. See Ab805.

Ad297a   Ad298, *ibid.*, pp.239–41. See Ac779, 797, 828, 829.

1939

Ac314a   Extract from Ab308 in *Victor Brauner*, Paris: Galerie Henriette, 19 mai — 5 juin 1939. [Exhib.cat.]

1940

Ab315a   Ab316.2 first published under title 'Ce qu'ils lisent', *Le Figaro littéraire*, CXV, 69 (9 mars 40), A. See Ac804.

1944

Ac358a   'Notice' in Gisèle Prassinos, *Le Feu maniaque*, Paris: R.J. Godet. See Aa447.

1945

Ab368a   'Thomas de Quincey (1784–1859)' [from Aa315], *Le Ciel bleu*, I, 1 (1 mars 45). See Ac794.*

Aa368b   Aa361 [abr.] in Portuguese under title 'A situaçâo do "Super-realismo" entre as duas guerras', *Afinidades* (Lisbon), 14/15 (dez.45), 33–39.

Ac370a   Ac355 in *Enrico Donati*, Paris: Galerie Drouant-David, 1946 [Exhib.cat.].*

1947

Ad403a   Ad397 in *Le Libertaire*, 78 (22 mai 47), 3. See Ac804, 815.

1948

Ad421a   Brief untitled texts on exclusion of Matta and Brauner from surrealist movement, *Néon*, 4 (nov.48). See Ac804.

Ad421b   'La Paix par nous-mêmes', *Le Franc-tireur*, VIII, 1356 (9 déc.48), 1, 3.

1949

Ab427a   'Égard (et gare) à l'impatience', *Peuple du monde* [suppl. of *Combat*], 3 (5 fév.49). See Ab812.

Ac439   Add:
.3 'Chaumont...', 2 lines sent to Valéry (24 juil.16). See Aa839.

Aa441a   *L'Amour fou* [Aa276], Paris: Gallimard, 1949. See Aa782.

1950

Ab453a   Ac460 under title 'La peinture: Michel G. Vivancos', *Le Libertaire*, 225 (21 avr.50), 3. See Ac815.

Ab455a   'Masques à transformation de la côte Pacifique du Nord-Ouest', *Neuf*, 1 (juin 50). See Ab821.*

Ad465a   'Les Intellectuels français demandent la grâce de Kalandra condamné à mort au procès des Treize à Prague', *Combat*, IX, 1851 (17–18 juin 50), 3. See Ac804.

Ac461   Add: Paris: Galerie des Beaux Arts, nov. 1950 [Exhib.cat.].*

1951

Ad480a   'Une Protestation justifiée...', *Le Libertaire*, 262 (30 mars 51), 3. See Ac804.

Ad480b   'Un Appel contre la répression', *Le Franc-tireur*, XI, 2063 (16 mars 51). See Ac804.

Ad482a   Ad481 under title 'Le Dernier Manifeste surréaliste', *Le Libertaire*, 276 (6 juil.51), 3. See Ac808.

Ad482b   Ad481a in Spanish under title 'Surrealistas y anarquistas', *Solidaridad obrera* (Paris), (20 oct.51), 4. See Ac779.

1952

Ab488a   ['Hitler, Mussolini y Stalin tuvierón en España'], *Solidaridad obrera* (1 mars 52), 1, 22 3.

Ad502a   Ad503 in *Le Libertaire*, 296 (4 jan.52), 3. See Ac804, Ac815.

Ad504   Journal ref.: *Le Libertaire*, 316 (23 mai 52), 3. See Ac779, Ac804, Ac815.

1953

Aa506.1   published in Ab293a. See Ab805.

1954

Ab538a   'Leçon d'octobre' [Ab545], *Combat-Art*, 4 (1 mars 54).

Ab548a   'Familier du Grand Truc' from Ad548 in *Potlatch*, 14 (30 nov.54).*

1956

Ad577a   *A cœur et à cri*, tract, Paris, Summer 56. See Ad764, Ac804.*

Ad577b   'Les surréalistes: "Les fascistes sont ceux qui tirent sur le peuple"', *Le Figaro littéraire*, XI, 552 (17 nov.56), 3. See Ac804.

Ad581a   Ad578 in *Le Franc-tireur*, XV, 3823 (10–11 nov.56), 7. See Ad711a, Ac808.

Ad581b   Ad578 in *Le Monde libertaire*, 23 (déc.56), 3.

1957

Ab584a   'Contre vents et marées...' [written on 40th anniversary of October Revolution], *La Vérité*, 477 (14 nov.57), 2–3. Replaces Ab713. See Ac779.

Ad591a   'Motion adressée au Juge Perez', *ibid.*, p.2.

1959

Ad620a   'Texte adressé à 99 intellectuels français (10 avril 59)', *Le Quatorze juillet*, 3 (10 avr.59), 1. See Ac804.

1960

Ad627a   *A vous de dire*, single sheet, Paris, 9 fév.1960. See Ac804.

Ad627b.1 'Riposte. La Bénédiction de l'un vaut l'autopsie de l'autre'.
Ad627b.2 Letter to M. Isarlo (Editor).
          in *Combat-Art*, 66 (4 avr.60), 1, 2. See Ac804.

Ad628a   Ad641 published under title 'Manifeste des 121', *New York Post* (14 Sept.60). See Ac804.*

Ad628b   'Message des surréalistes aux intellectuels polonais', (4 juin 59), *Front unique*, 2 (aut./oct.60). See Ac804.*

Ad631a   Ad630 under title 'Affaire close pour le principal des poètes', *Le Figaro littéraire*, 765 (17 déc.60), 11.

Ac631b   Ab37.1 & .2, 41, 105b in *391* [facsimile reprint], Paris: Le Terrain Vague, 1960.

1961

Ad634a   'Lamentable exposition "surréaliste"', *Combat-Art*, 81 (4 sept.61).

1962

Ad656a   'Boussole', *Combat-Art*, 87 (5 mars 62), 2. See Ac804.

1963

Aa660a [With Tanguy] *Volière*, 1963 (15 mai). 250 copies (nos I-XXII contain 'Avant-dire' autographed by AB and original drawing by Tanguy). Facsimile reproduction of handwritten texts. Contains: Aa221.9; Ab1.3, 3, 10, 11, 12, 38 under title 'Poses fatales'[as in Aa195], 68.2, 'Étoile' [Extract from Ab53], 70, 93.2, 239, 317, 344.6; Ac439.2, 439.3.

Ad665a [With Edouard Jaguer & José Pierre] 'A vos rangs, fixe', *Combat-Art*, 99–100 (30 avr.–6 mai 63). See Ac804.

Ac676 Add: Bilingual cat. French at one end, with 1 extra sentence; English at other end, upside down, tr. W.G. Ryan. Text dated 16 fév.63.

1964

Ad688a Ad 680 in José Pierre, 'Cramponnez-vous à la table (Petite suite surréaliste à l'affaire du Bazar Charpentier')', *Le Petit Ecrason*, 2 (1964), 2–5. See Ac804.

1965

Ad699a *Le 'Troisième degré' de la peinture*, single sheet, Paris, 6 oct.1965. See Ac804.

1966

Ab708a 'A la croisée des chemins' [written c. 1920], in Michel Sanouillet, 'Le Dossier de *Dadaglobe*', *Cahiers pour l'Association internationale pour l'étude de dada et du surréalisme*, 1 (oct.66), 142–43. Published as anonymous. See Aa839.

Ad708b   *Ni aujourd'hui ni de cette manière* (19 avr.66). See Ac768, 779.*

Ac709a   Ab104 [quoted in full] in Clara Malraux, *Le Bruit de nos pas II. Nos vingt ans*, Paris: Grasset, 1966.

Ac711   Also includes Ab691.1.*

Ad711a   Ad578 in *Le Monde libertaire*, 126 (nov.66), 1. This page also includes photograph of hand holding card: 'AB est mort. Aragon est vivant... C'est un double malheur pour la pensée honnête.'

1967

Ab713   Replaced by Ab584a.

Ac717a   Ab20 [facsimile of MS] in Aragon, 'Lautréamont et nous', *Les Lettres françaises* (1–7 juin 67). See Ac786.*

1968

Ac721a   Ad125, 126, 127, 149, 184, 185, 192, 193, 194, 234 and 236 in Paul Éluard, *Œuvres complètes*, II, Paris: Gallimard (Bibl. de la Pléiade), 1968.

1969

Ac723a   *Paravent pour les douze mois de l'année*, Paris: Guy Lévis Mano, GLM, nov.1969, 225 copies. Includes one sentence by AB.

1971

Ac743a   Ac645 in new edn, Paris: Gallimard (Coll. 'Idées'), 1971.

Ac743b   Ac702 in new edn, Paris: UGE (Coll. '10/18') 1971.

A : PRIMARY MATERIAL

(ii) Publications 1972–1989

1972

Aa744   *Position politique du surréalisme* [Aa235], Paris: Denoël/Gonthier (Coll. 'Médiations'), 177pp.

Aa745   *La Claire Tour* [Ab485], n.p.: J.-L. Thuillier, 1972. Presented as unpubl.text. See Ac779, Ac815.

Aa746   *Manifestes du surréalisme* [Aa666], Paris: Pauvert, 1972, 317pp. See Aa817, Aa839.

Aa747   *Nadja* [Aa683], Paris: Gallimard (Coll. 'Folio', 73), 1972, 190pp. See Aa839.

Ab748   Ab243 in *Le Surréalisme. 1922–42*, Musée des Arts Décoratifs, 1972 [Exhib.cat.].

1973

Ab749.1   Letters to Paul Nougé (oct.26–avr.33). Letter dated 25 mai 27 also in Aa707.

Ab749.2   Letters to Camille Gœmans (10 avr.29–18 mai 30).
In *Lettres surréalistes, Le fait accompli*, 81–95 (mai–août 73), Brussels: Les Lèvres Nues.

Ac750   Letter as postface in Paul Laraque, *Ce qui demeure*, Montreal: Nouvelle Optique, 1973.*

Ad751   *De la jurisprudence surréaliste*, 1 sheet, with photographs. Brussels: Les Lèvres Nues, 1973.

Aa752   *Martinique charmeuse de serpents* [Aa404], Paris: UGE (Coll. '10/18'), 1973, 114pp.

Aa753   *Entretiens* [Aa484], Paris: Gallimard (Coll. 'Idées', 284), 1973.

Aa754   *La Clé des champs* [Aa506], Paris: UGE (Coll. '10/18'), 440pp.

Ab755   Ab379 in *Soundings* (Spring 73), 1–6.*

1974

Ab756   Letter to André Derain (3 oct.21), in Werner Spies, *Max Ernst — Collagen, Inventar und Widerspruch*, Cologne: M. DuMont Schauberg, 1974; also tr. under title *Max Ernst. Les Collages. Inventaire et contradictions*, tr. Eliane Kaufholz, Paris: Gallimard, 1984.

Ac757   'Le Pinceau de l'amour' [written in 1922], in *Les Tours Eiffel de Robert Delaunay*, Brussels: Robert de Velder, 1974 (1150 copies), pp.53–56. See Aa839.

Ac758   (Previously unpubl. texts from *Poisson soluble*)
Ac758.1 'Le soleil est un chien basset...'. See Aa839.
Ac758.2 'J'ai toujours été condamné...'. See Aa839.
Ac758.3 'Poème avec vocabulaire'.
Ac758.4 'Poème exhibitionniste'.
Ac758.5 'Poème fin du monde'.
         In Sarane Alexandrian, *Le Surréalisme et le rêve*, Paris: Gallimard, 1974.

Ac760   Ac26, Extract from Ab88, Aa277.1 under title 'Jacques Vaché. 1895–1919', Ab413 and extract from Aa315, in Arthur Cravan, Jacques Rigaut, Jacques Vaché, *Trois suicidés de la société*, Paris: Eric Losfeld/UGE (Coll. '10/18'), 1974.

Ad761   Ad125 in *Le Surréalisme contestataire et contesté*, *Points et contrepoints*, 113 (déc.74), 6–7. See Ac797.

1975

Ab762   'Texte de Breton écrit pour la *Literaturnaja Gazeta* à la demande de Romoff' (18 juil.32), *Cahiers du vingtième siècle*, 4 (1975), 155–57. Introduction by Jean-Charles Gateau and Georges Nivat, see Bb1072.

Ab763   'Où en est le surréalisme?' (1953), *La Vie des arts* (Montreal), XX, 80 (aut.75), 16–17. See At951. Extracts from this radio programme were published in *La Semaine à Radio-Canada*, III, 17 (1–7 fév.53), 5–6.

Ad764   Ad577a in *1122*, suppl. of *Mai hors saison* (1975–76), 22. See Ac804.*

Ac765   *Le Cadavre exquis, son exaltation* [Ac418], Arturo Schwarz, ed., with texts by Juidrich Chalupecky and others, Saint-Etienne: Musée d'Art et d'Industrie, Feb.1975 [Exhib.cat.].

Ac766   Aa129(Ab139); Ab106, 112, 113, 114, 116, 117, 118, 120, 121, 127c(105c), 131, 132, 133, 134, 142, 143, 156, 157, 158, 159, 167, 168, 169; Ad124, 127, 137(Ab138), 136(Ab140), and 150(153).
In *La Révolution surréaliste* [facsimile reprint], Paris: Jean-Michel Place, 1972.

Ac767   Ab540 in José Pierre, *Max Walter Svanberg et le règne féminin*, Paris: Le Musée de Poche, 1975.*

1976

Ab768.1   'Certifié sans la moindre retouche...'(juin 53). Photograph of note on automatic sentences, handwritten on copy of *Les Champs magnétiques*.
Ab768.2   'Ouvrez-vous?'. MS of AB's replies to surrealist game.
Ab768.3   MS note on distribution of artists for exhibition Ac640.
Ab768.4   Facsimile of draft reply to survey on empty pedestals in occupied Paris.

Ab768.5   Facsimile of announcement of first issue of *Le Surréalisme même* (1956).
Also includes photograph of MS pages of Ab41, 34, 623; facsimile of MS used as frontispiece for Aa141; photograph of AB's handwritten corrections on draft of first page of Ad577; Ab662a.
In Gérard Legrand, *AB en son temps*, Paris: Le Soleil Noir, 1976.

Ac769   Letter to Edouard Autant (21 fév.19), in Michel Corvin, *Le Théâtre de recherche entre les deux guerres. Le laboratoire art et action*, Lausanne: La Cité/l'Age d'Homme, 1976, p.449.

Ac770   Letter (22 jan.66) as postface in Oleg Ibrahimoff, *Le Prince Oleg et autres dits*, Paris: Éditions St Germain des Prés, 1976.

Aa771   *L'Amour fou* [A276], Paris: Gallimard (Coll 'Folio', 723), 1976. See Aa782.

Ab772   Ab104 under title 'Quand *Les Nouvelles littéraires* défendaient le rebelle (16 août 24)', *Les Nouvelles littéraires*, LIII, 2560 (25 nov.–1 déc.76), 6. See Aa839.

Ab773   Bb194, under title '31 juillet 1958. Poésie 58. AB' [interview with Pierre de Boisdeffre], *Les Nouvelles littéraires*, LIII, 2514 (5 jan.76), 20–21.

Ac774   Ab177, 178, 179, 180, 181, 182, 187.1 and .2, 188, 189, 190, 204, 205, 206, 207 and 208.
In *Le Surréalisme au service de la révolution* [facsimile reprint], Paris: Jean-Michel Place, 1976.

Ac775   Ab327 in André Masson, *Rebelle du surréalisme. Écrits*, Paris: Hermann (Coll. 'Savoir'), 1976, pp.227–33.

1977

Ac776   Ab93.3 and also
Ac776.1   'Pour Denise' [4 poems]. See Aa839.
In Pierre Naville, *Le Temps du surréel*, Paris: Galilée, 1977.

Ac777   Ab615 in *Antonin Artaud, La Tour de feu*, 136 (déc.77), 5–7.

Ac778   Ac656 in new edn, Paris: Minuit, 1977.

Ac779   Aa506.1; Ab121, 237, 309, 376, 431, 454, 455, 485, 491, 492, 512, 623, 648; Ad234, 266, 273, 287, 298, 481a, 504, 584a (Ab713) under title 'La Révolution d'octobre', and Ad708b.
In Arturo Schwarz, *AB, Trotsky et l'anarchie*, Paris: UGE (Coll. '10/18', 1174), 1977.

1978

Aa780   *Deux Poèmes. 1914*, Montpellier, Fata Morgana n.d. [1978], unpag. [3], 19 copies. Contains Ab9 and also:

Aa780.1   'Dire à voir cette main' [full text of Ac439.1]. See Ab790, Aa795, Aa839.

Ab781   Letter from AB to Fernand Leduc (17 sept.43) [Extract], in Jean Chatard, 'Automatisme et surréalisme au Québec', *Le Puits de l'ermite*, 28–30–31 (mars 78), 148–52.

Aa782   *L'Amour fou* [Aa276], Paris: Gallimard, 1978, 133pp.

Aa783   *Almanach surréaliste du demi-siècle* [Aa446] [facsimile reprint], Paris: Plasma, 1978.

Ab784   Letter to Grégoire Michonze (25 jan.50), *Les Cahiers bleus*, 13 (aut.78), 76–77.

Ab785   Ab70 presented by Dawn Ades as 'A Breton inédit', *Adam International Review*, XLI, 404–06 (1978), 31–32. Includes a facsimile reproduction of MS. See Ac786, 797, Aa839.

Ac786   Ab17, 18, 20, 21, 22, 23, 24, 25, 30, 31, 33, 47, 48, 49, 53, 54, 57, 59, 63, 64, 65, 66, 70, 70a, 72, 73, 74, 75, 76, 77, 78, 79, 86, 87, 91.
In *Littérature* [facsimile reprint], Paris: Jean-Michel Place, 1978.

Ac787   Ac505 in new edn, Vanves: Édn. Thot, 1978. See Ac800.

Ac788   Ab105b in Francis Picabia, *Écrits*, II, Paris: Belfond, 1978.

1979

Ab789.1   Letter to Magritte (10 mars 36).

Ab789.2   Letters to E.L.T. Mesens (21 sept.38, 18 fév.57).
In *Lettres mêlées* (1920–1966), Brussels: Les Lèvres Nues, 1979.

Ab790   Aa780.1, *Création*, XV (15 juin 79). See Ab795, Aa839.*

Ac791   Ac466 in new edn, Paris: Gallimard, 1979.*

Ab792   Ac570 under title 'Man Ray', *Adam International Review*, 419–21 (1979), 13.
Date of original publ. given as 1916 instead of 1956.

Ac793   Letters to Alain Bosquet (3.6.42, 18.3.43) [from Ab722], in *Alain Bosquet*,
Paris: Belfond (Coll. 'Identités'), 1979, pp.137–39.

Ac794   Facsimiles of Ab161, 164, 226, 316.1, 316.2, 368a; Ac214; Ad126a, 127 and
203, in Marcel Mariën, ed., *L'Activité surréaliste en Belgique (1924–1950)*,
Brussels: Édns Lebeer-Hossmann & Paris: Bibl. des Arts (Coll. 'Le Fil rouge').

1980

Aa795   *L'An suave: neuf poèmes et une prose de mil-neuf-cent-quatorze*,
Montpellier: Fata Morgana, Bibl artistique et littéraire, 1980,
unpag., 222 copies. Contains Ab1.1, 1.2, 1.3, 3, 4, 9, 14,
Aa780.1 (Ab790), and also:

Aa795.1   'Camaïeu' [written c. 1914, last stanza later broken up as Ab39].
See Aa839.

Aa795.2   'L'Eau douce' [written oct.14]. See Aa839.

Aa796   Letter from AB to Blanche Derval, and photograph of dedication
of *Le Manifeste du surréalisme* and *Nadja*, in G.L.,
Nadja/Blanche, plaquette [4pp], n.d. [1980].

Ac797.1   [With Vitrac, Desnos, Éluard, Aragon, Morise] Letter to Clément
Vautel (6 août 23).

Ac797.2   'Lettre à nos amis de Londres' (21 oct.38), signed 'Le Groupe
surréaliste'.

Ac797.3 'Lettre ouverte à M. Camille Chautemps...' (7 août 37).
Ac797.4 'Carte postale au Général Gouraud' (mars 30).
Ac797.5 Letter to 'l'Université de Paris' (18 déc.21).
Also contains Aa197; Ab70, 115, 126, 158, 164, 298; Ac108 (dated 22 août 24), 214, 284; Ad97a, 108a, 109, 109a, 110.1, 110a, 111d, 126a, 126b, 126c, 127a, 127b, 127e, 137 (dated 18 mai 26), 148, 149, 125, 150, 151, 161, 184, 185, 190a under title 'Lettre ouverte à l'Ambassadeur de Chine à Paris', 191, 192, 193, 194, 213, 215.2, 215a, 216, 232, 234, 249, 252, 254, 266, 267, 267a, 269, 271, 272, 273, 287 under title 'Discours d'AB à propos du second Procès de Moscou', 291, 299, 300, 311, 312, 313, — in José Pierre, *Tracts surréalistes et déclarations collectives 1922–1969. Tome I: 1922–1939*, Paris : Losfeld/Le Terrain Vague, 1980.

Ac798 Letter to Marcel Havrenne (1 nov.35), in *Le Surréalisme en Hainault*, La Louvière: Institut des Arts et Métiers, 1979; Paris: Centre Culturel de la Communauté Française de Belgique, mars 1980; Marseille, oct.80, pp.118–19 [Exhib.cat.].*

Ac799 Ab2, 4, 6, 7, 12 in *Nord-Sud* [facsimile reprint], Paris: Jean-Michel Place, 1980.

Ac800 Ac505 in new edn, Geneva: Slatkine, 1980.

1981

Ac801 Letters to Rosenberg (15 & 27 déc.18, 11 juin 19), in Piero Pacini, 'Intorno al numero cubista di *Valori plastici*', *Critica d'arte*, XLVI, n.s., 175–77 (genn.–giugno 81). Letters from Severini Archives, Rome.

Ac802 Ac574 in new edn, Paris: Jean Picollec, 1981.

31

1982

Ab803   'Déclaration d'AB au meeting du P.O.I. en décembre 1936' (17 déc.36), in *Cahiers Léon Trotsky*, 9 (jan.82), 113–14.

Ac804.1 [With Péret] 'Clôture définitive des affaires Carrouges et Pastoureau'.
Ac804.2 'Étoile double. Lettre à un groupe de militants' (oct.52). See Ac816.
Ac804.3 'Qui après Paul Fort?'.
Ac804.4 [With Benayoun, Legrand, Mesens, Schuster] Letter to André Parinaud (30 mars 60).
Ac804.5 Letter to PCI, French section (20 oct.65).
Ac804.6 [With Audoin, Bounoure, Legrand, Pierre, Schuster] 'A la Presse' (19 avr.66).
Ac804.7 Letters (1951).
Ac804.8 'Tranchons-en' (déc.65).
Ac804.9 'Appel en faveur d'un cercle international des intellectuels révolutionnaires'; and also:
Aa421, 440, Aa506.2; Ab316.2, 428, 452, 455, 467, 540, 552, 566; Ac349, 601, 620, 679; Ad397, 398, 421a, 465a, 480, 480a under title 'Lettre à la rédaction', 480b under title 'Contre la répression en Catalogne', 481, 481a, 481b, 503, 504, 576, 577, 577a, 577b, 592, 603, 620a, 627a, 628, 628b, 629, 630, 641, 642, 656a, 664, 665, 665a, 680, 681, 699a — in José Pierre, *Tracts surréalistes et déclarations collectives 1922–1969. Tome II: 1940–1969*, Paris: Losfeld/Le Terrain Vague, 1982.

Ab805   Ab293a [Aa506.1] in *Cahiers Léon Trotsky*, 12 (déc.82), 105–18.

Ac806   Ab317, 331 [in French], Ac145, 294, in *Yves Tanguy. Rétrospective 1925–1955*, Paris: Centre Georges Pompidou, 17 juin–27 sept.82 [Exhib.cat.].

Ac807   Ab467 in Goutier, Jean-Michel, ed., *Benjamin Péret*, Paris: Henri Veyrier, 1982. Also contains drawing by AB for 'Le grand jeu de Benjamin Péret' and dedication from AB to Péret.

Ac808   Ad481, 481a and 578, [facsimile reprod.] in Pietro Ferrua, *Surréalisme et anarchisme*, Paris: Le Monde Libertaire, 1982.

1983

Ab809   4 texts from 'Le Pagure dit' in *Les Champs magnétiques*, not in original publication:
Ab809.1 'Costume-tailleur'. See Aa839.
Ab809.2 'De fil en aiguille'. See Aa839.
Ab809.3 'Haltères'. See Aa839.
Ab809.4 'Rectifications'. See Aa839.
         Also contains:
Ab809.5 Letter to Fraenkel (3 juin 16).
Ab809.6 Drawing-text (1916).
         In *Permanence du surréalisme*, *Digraphe*, 30 (juin 83).

Ad810   *Le Jeu de Marseille*, Marseille: André Dimanche, 1983.

Aa811   *Anthologie de l'humour noir* [Aa447], Paris: Livre de Poche, 1984, 446pp. See Aa852.

Ab812   Ab416 (text corrected by Marguerite Bonnet and José Pierre), Ab427a and Ab489 in *Champs des activités surréalistes (CAS)*, 17, n.s. (fév.83).

Ac813   Ac627 in new edn, Grenoble: Presses Universitaires de Grenoble (Coll. 'Débuts d'un siècle').

Ad814   'Déclaration commune' [Extract from Ad253], in C.B. Morris, *El manifiesto surrealista escrito en Tenerife*, Tenerife: Instituto de Estudios Canarios, Univ. de la Laguna, 1983.*

Ac815   Ab431, 485, 489, 491, Ac460, Ad397, 481a, 503, 504, Ad804.2 in José Pierre, *Surréalisme et anarchie*. Les 'billets surréalistes' du 'Libertaire' (12 oct.1951–8 jan.1953), Paris: Plasma (Coll. 'En Dehors'), 1983.

1985

Ab816   Letter (15 déc.50) in *Catalogue de la Librairie de l'Échiquier*, 71 [1985].*

Aa817   *Manifestes du surréalisme* [Ad666], Paris: Gallimard (Coll. 'Folio'). See Aa839.

Aa818   *Farouche à quatre feuilles* [Aa533], Paris: Grasset (Coll. 'Les Cahiers Rouges'), 1985.

Ab819   Ab10 and 11 in new edn of *Les Trois Roses*, Bibliothèque de Vercheny: Édn. Grande Nature, 1985.

Ab820   Ab387 in *Les Deux Sœurs* [facsimile reprint], Paris: Jean-Michel Place, 1985.

Ab821   Ab455a and Ab168 (under title 'Paul Valéry corrigé par AB et Paul Éluard', with Valéry's text alongside), *Pleine marge*, 1 (1985). Introduction by Marie-Paule Berranger, see Bb878. See Aa839.

1986

Ab822   'Les pages marquées de craie...' [written 1919], *Modernités*, 1 (1986), 11. See Aa839.

Ab823.1 'Réunion du 23 janvier 1925 au Bar Certa'. See Aa839.
Ab823.2 'Jeanne d'Arc' (Letter, with facsimile of MS) (31 mars 26). In *Luna-park*, 8–9 (1986). See Aa839.

Ab824   'Deux lettres inédites à Fernand Demoustier dit Dumont' (24 juin, 7 juil.33), *L'Orne littéraire*, 10 (1986), 88–89.

Ac825   Letter to René Gaffé (3 nov.32), in Arthur Cravan, *Œuvres. Poèmes, articles, lettres*, Paris: Gérard Lebovici, 1987, p.216.

Aa826   *Qu'est-ce que le surréalisme?* [Aa218], Paris: Actual & Cognac: Le Temps qu'il fait, 1986.

Ab827   Ab121 in *Trotsky et les écrivains français*, *Cahiers Léon Trotsky*, 25 (mars 86), 19–22. See Aa839.

Ac828   Ad298 in *Los Surrealistas en Mexico*, Mexico City: Museo Nacional de Arte, 1986 [Exhib.cat.]. See Ac830.*

Ac829   Ad298 in Gérard Roche, 'Breton, Trotsky: une collaboration', *Pleine marge*, 3 (mai 86), 76–84. Includes AB's original project for text.

Ad830   Ad548 in Gérard Berreby, ed., *Documents relatifs à la fondation de l'Internationale Situationniste*, Paris: Allia, 1985, pp.274, 276 and 187–88.

1987

Aa831   *A vous seule. Poème inédit par AB. Suivi d'une lettre à l'auteur par Paul Valéry*, Montpellier: Fata Morgana, n.d. [1987]. 79 copies. See Aa839.

Ab832   Letter to Gala (16 avr.30), in Erika Billeter and José Pierre, eds., *La Femme et le surréalisme*, Lausanne: Musée Cantonal des Beaux-Arts, 1987, p.22.

Ad833   '"La Femme selon l'optique surréaliste" d'AB, Vincent Bounoure, Radovan Ivsic, Joyce Mansour, José Pierre: un projet d'exposition avorté', *ibid.*, pp.465–71.

Ab834   Ab386 in *Pleine marge*, 6 (déc.87), 87–88.

Ab835   Ab59 in Marguerite Bonnet, *L'Affaire Barrès*, Paris: Corti (Coll. 'Actual'). See Aa839.

Ac836   Aa406.3 in Ferrari, ed., *Entretiens morphologiques. Notebook No 1. 1936–1944*, I, London: Sistan, 1987.*

Ac837   Ac502 (facsimile of MS letter) in *Arc-en-ciel. Francis Picabia*, Galerie 1900/2000, 1987 [Exhib.cat.].

Ac838   Aa726.3 in Marie-Claire Dumas, ed., *Robert Desnos*, Paris: Cahiers de l'Herne, 1987.

1988

Aa839   *Œuvres complètes*, I, Marguerite Bonnet, ed. [with Philippe Bernier, Étienne-Alain Hubert, José Pierre], Paris: Gallimard (Bibl. de la Pléiade), 1988, 1798pp. Contains three chronological sections:

[i] 1911–1919: *Mont de piété* [Aa15], Aa795.1 and .2, 833; Ab1.1, Ab1.2, 1.3, 1a.1, 1a.2, 5, 7, 8, 14, 18, 780; Ac439.2 and .3
and also:

Aa839.1 'Lorsque tout dort...'.
Aa839.2 'Rondel'.
Aa839.3 'Portrait étrange'.
Aa839.4 ['Ris, poste...'].
Aa839.5 ['Des terrasses du Songe...'].
Aa839.6 ['Comme une châsse d'or...'].
Aa839.7 'Vers une fin d'été'.
Aa839.8 'Couleur d'heure'.
Aa839.9 ['Le regret des soleils...'].
Aa839.10 'Coquito'.
Aa839.11 ['Immeubles démolis...'].
Aa839.12 'Soldat'.
Aa839.13 'Quelles sont nos garanties?'.

[ii] 1920–1924: *Les Champs magnétiques* [Aa29], *Clair de terre* [Aa85], *Les Pas perdus* [Aa98], *Manifeste du surréalisme. Poisson soluble* [Aa99]; 'Phrases' (single sentences publ. in Dada reviews), Ab33, 42a, 44, 47, 53, 58, 59, 70a, 74, 76, 87, 97, 100, 101.1, 101a, 104, 105, 105c (under title 'Communiqué sur le Bureau de recherches surréalistes'), 708a, 823, 824.1; Ac108, 757 (under title 'A Robert Delaunay', with slight variants), 758.1 and .2, 776; Ad82 (under title 'Appel du 3 janvier 1922');
and also:

Aa839.14 'Le Pagure dit:' [II]. 4 of these texts were previously published in Ab809.

Aa839.15 'Concours de circonstances'.
Aa839.16 ['A temps nouveaux...'].
Aa839.17 'Brique de cinamome'.
Aa839.18 'Chansons internationales'.
Aa839.19 'Mairie américaine'.
Aa839.20 'Tapis lisible'.
Aa839.21 ['Le jeu de barres...'].
Aa839.22 ['J'ai vu un coq...'].
Aa839.23 ['Une femme c'était...'].
Aa839.24 ['Roulades...'].
Aa839.25 ['Par le froid...'].
Aa839.26 ['Sans cérémonie...'].
Aa839.27 ['Les supplices paresseux...'].
Aa839.28 ['Le doux paquet...'].
Aa839.29 ['Un mouchoir noir...'].
Aa839.30 ['Épiphanie de l'amour...'].
Aa839.31 ['L'enfant aux cheveux de bristol...'].
Aa839.32 *Poisson soluble* [II].
Aa839.33 'Poème destiné à être lu au mariage de T. Fraenkel'.
Aa839.34 ['Ah fini de courir'].
Aa839.35 ['L'embarquement...'] (6 poems).
Aa839.36 ['Tu es grave...'].
Aa839.37 'Paul Éluard'.
Aa839.38 'Philippe Soupault'.
Aa839.39 'Carnet' (1920–1921).
Aa839.40 'Les "Enfers artificiels". Ouverture de la "Saison dada 1921"' (1921).
Aa839.41 [With Aragon] ['Projet pour la bibliothèque de Jacques Doucet']. Letter to Jacques Doucet (fév.21). Extracts quoted in Bb973.
Aa839.42 ['Mise en accusation d'Arthur Meyer'].

[iii] 1925–1930: revised edn of *Nadja* [Aa155] as in Aa660, *Ralentir travaux* [Aa174], *Second Manifeste du surréalisme* [Aa175], *L'Immaculée Conception* [Aa176]; Ab106, 112, 113, 114, 114a, 115, 116, 120, 121, 122, 123, 130, 156, 158, 164,

165, 168, 169, 179, Ab824.2 (under title ['Oh Monsieur, quelle femme...']); Ac182a; Ad137, 148, 149, 160, 184, 185; and also:

Aa839.43 ['Avant une Conférence de Jean Genbach'].
Aa839.44 'Le Chapelet des aiguilles'.
Aa839.45 'Le Masque du jour'.
Aa839.46 ['Le rouge est assez aéré...'].
Aa839.47 ['Tu n'es pas...'].
Aa839.48 ['Les toits de briques...'].
Aa839.49 'Vernissage'.
Aa839.50 ['La taillerie de diamants...'].
Aa839.51 ['C'est un rosier...'].
Aa839.52 ['L'idée de l'amour...'].
Aa839.53 ['Je dépenserai toujours bien...'].
Aa839.54 ['La porte de la maison de Lise...'].
Aa839.55 ['C'est toi ce n'est pas nous...'].
Aa839.56 ['Lumière ai-je dit...'].
Aa839.57 ['Je ne sais pas mais je sais...'].
Aa839.58 ['Mes pas dans les tiens...'].
Aa839.59 ['Du temps que les choses parlaient...'].
Aa839.60 ['Fais que le jour...'].

Ab840   Letters to Enrico Donati (1945–49) in *Pleine marge*, 7 (juin 88), 13–26. Includes Ac435.

Ac841.1 Letters to Jacques Doucet (1921–24). Extracts quoted in Bb973.
Ac841.2 Letter to Picasso (mars/avr.24).
In *Les Demoiselles d'Avignon*, Vol.II, Paris: Éditions de la Réunion des Musées Nationaux, 1988, pp.583–91.

Ad842   Entries by AB, in Paule Thévenin, ed., *Bureau de recherches surréalistes. Cahier de la permanence. Octobre 1924–avril 1925*, Paris: Gallimard (Archives du Surréalisme, 1), 1988.

Ad843   Entries by AB, in Marguerite Bonnet, *Vers l'Action politique. De 'La Révolution d'abord et toujours!' (juillet 1925) au projet de*

'La Guerre civile' (avril 1926), Paris: Gallimard (Archives du Surréalisme, 2), 1988.

Aa844   *Les Champs magnétiques* [Aa29], Paris: Lachenal et Ritter, 1988, 257pp. Facsimile reproduction and transcription of original MS, notes and presentation by Serge Fauchereau, and introduction by Lydie Lachenal.

Aa845   *De la survivance de certains mythes et de quelques autres mythes en croissance ou en formation* [Ac337], Paris: Losfeld/Terrain Vague, 1988, 27pp. Postface by José Pierre.

Ac846   Ac547 in new edn, Paris: Jean-Jacques Pauvert (Coll. 'Le Désordre'), 1988.

1989

Aa847   *Lumière du jour*, Paris: Actual, 1989. 300 copies.*

Ab848   Letters to Marie-Louise Vaché, in Jacques Vaché, *79 Lettres de guerre*, Paris: Jean-Michel Place, 1989.*

Ac849   Collage (13 jan. 1919) [facsimile reprod.], in Georges Sebbag, *L'Imprononçable Jour de sa mort Jacques Vaché janvier 1919*, Paris: Jean-Michel Place, 1989.

Aa850   *Ralentir travaux* [Aa174], Paris: Corti, 1989, 84pp. Presentation by Jean-Claude Mathieu.

Aa851   *Arcane 17* [Aa382], Paris: Livre de Poche (Coll. 'Biblio'), 1989.

Aa852   *Anthologie de l'humour noir* [Aa447], Paris: Livre de Poche (Coll. 'Biblio'), 1989.

1936

At946   'Rather Life' [Aa85.7], 'The Plume' [Aa85.12], 'Allotropy' [Ab134.2], 'The Vertebrate Sphinx' [Aa195.14], tr. Denis Devlin, in 'Four Poems', *Contemporary Poetry and Prose* (London), 4–5 (Aug.–Sept.36), 82–55*; reprinted in Denis Devlin, *Collected Poems* edited by J.C.C. Mays, Dublin: Dedalus, 1989, pp.116–22.

1968

At947   'Towards an Independent Revolutionary Art' [Ad298], in Herschel B. Chipp, *Theories of Modern Art*, Berkeley, Los Angeles & London: Univ. of California Press, 1968.

1972

At948   *Surrealism and Painting*, tr. S.W. Taylor, New York: Harper & Row, London: MacDonald, 1972.

At949   At939 in new edn, Ann Arbor Paperback, 1972.

1974

At950   'What is Surrealism?', tr. David Gascoyne, New York: Haskell House Publ., 1974.*

1975

At951 'Towards a Free Revolutionary Art' [Ad298], in Leon Trotsky, *Culture and Socialism and a Manifesto: Towards a Free Revolutionary Art*, tr. Dwight Macdonald, London: New York Publ., 1975.

1977

At952 'The Pearl is marred, in my eyes...'[Ac354], and 'Three years ago...' [Ac394.1] [extracts from At949], in *Matta Coïgitum*, London: Hayward Gallery (27 Sept.–20 Nov.77) [Exhib.cat.].

1978

At953 'As in a Wood' [Ab472], in Paul Hammond, ed., *The Shadow and Its Shadow, Surrealist Writings on Cinema*, London: BFI, 1978, pp. 42–43.

At954 Rosemont, Franklin, *AB. What is Surrealism? Selected Writings*, New York: Monad and London: Pluto Press, 1978.

1980

At955 'The Faces of Women' [Ac231], 'Man Ray' [Ab570], and 'Convulsionists' [Ac286], in Janus, ed., *Man Ray: The Photographic Image*, London & Bedford: Gordon Fraser Gallery, 1980.

1982

At956   *Poems of AB: A Bilingual Anthology*, tr. and ed. Jean-Pierre Cauvin and Mary Ann Caws, pref. by Mary Ann Caws, introd. Jean-Pierre Cauvin, see Bb956, Austin: Univ of Texas Press, 1982, 260pp. Contains trans. (with facing French text) of: Aa 15.2, 15.3, 85.2, 85.10, 85.14, 99.2(exts), 186, 195.4, 195.6, 195.7, 195.10, 195.12, 195.13, 195.14, 195.15, 195.16, 195.18, 195.19, 221.1, 221.3, 221.5, 221.7, 221.10, 321, 406.1, 406.2, 406.3, 406.4, 406.5, 406.6, 605.2, 605.5, 632(ext); Ab 10, 19, 62.1, 62.2, 68.1, 86.3, 92.2, 93.2, 93.6, 96.2, 131.2, 229.2, 229.3, 229.4, 344.6, 347.1, 347.2, 347.3, 347.4, 347.6, 347.7, 352(ext), 387, 409, 609.2, 609.3, 611.2, 611.3, 611.4, 611.5, 612; Ac380, 417.2, 417.3, 417.4.

1985

At957   *The Magnetic Fields* [Aa29], tr. and introd. by David Gascoyne, London: Atlas Press, 1985, 111pp, 300 copies.

1986

At958   *Mad Love*, tr. and introd. by Mary Ann Caws, Lincoln & London: Univ. of Nebraska Press, 1986.

1987

At959   'If you Please' [Ab53], in Mel Gordon, ed., *Dada Performance*, New York: PAJ Publ., 1987.*

B: SECONDARY MATERIAL

a. Books and numbers of periodicals wholly or substantially devoted to Breton.

Ba7   Also translated under title *AB and the Basic Concepts of Surrealism*, tr. Maura Prendergast, Univ. of Alabama Press, 1974, 294pp.

Ba38   Albertazzi, Ferdinando, ed., *AB, un uomo attento*, Ravenna: Longo (Il Portico. Biblioteca di lettere et arti), 1971, 213pp. See Bb816, 867, 965, 1002, 1065, 1216, 1244, 1323, 1357, 1416, 1441, 1447, 1451, 1474.

Ba39   ——, *Biographie d'AB, poète*, Nice: J. Matarasso, 1983, unpag. [10pp.].

Ba40   Asari, Makoto, *AB et le sacré. Essai selon quelques thèmes religieux*, Paris: Publ. de l'Université Paris III–Sorbonne Nouvelle, 1984, 111pp.

Ba41   Aspley, Keith, *AB the Poet*, Glasgow: University of Glasgow French and German Publications, 1989, 236pp.

Balakian, Anna & R. Kuentz, see Ba53.

Ba42   Batache, Eddy, *Surréalisme et tradition: la pensée d'AB jugée selon l'œuvre de René Guénon*, Paris: Édns Traditionnelles, 1978, 174pp.

Ba43   ——, *Les Pensées d'AB*, Lausanne: L'Age d'Homme (Bibliothèque Mélusine), 1988, 362pp.

Ba44   Binni, Lanfranco, *AB*, Florence: La Nuova Italia (Il Castoro, 53), 1971, 147pp.*

Ba45   Bonnet, Marguerite, *AB. Naissance de l'aventure surréaliste*, Paris: Corti, 1975, 460pp. Revised edn, 1988, 464pp.

Ba46   ——, *Les Critiques de notre temps et Breton*, Paris: Garnier, 1974, 190pp. Contains extracts from Ba1, Ba3, 5, 14, 479; shortened versions of Bb159, 189, 274, 418, Bb823, Bb982; and in full Bb100, 164, 286a, 358, 379, 455, 536, 581, 626, 635, 710, 738. Also contains Maurice Blanchot, 'Quelques réflexions sur le surréalisme', first published in *Arche*, 8 (août 45) (not listed).

Ba47   ——, & Jacqueline Chénieux-Gendron, *Revues surréalistes françaises autour d'AB, 1948–1972*, Millwood, New York, London, Neudeln: Kraus International Publications, 1982, 294pp.

Ba48   Cardinal, Roger, *Breton: 'Nadja'*, London: Grant & Cutler (Critical Guides to French Texts, 60), 1986, 85pp.

Ba49   Cardoza y Aragon, Luis, *AB atisbado sin la mesa parlante*, Mexico: Universidad nacional autónoma de México, 1982.*

Ba50   ——, *Signos: Picasso, Breton y Artaud*, Mexico: Marcha Editores (Coll. 'El Circulo de Tizatl'), 1982.*

           Chénieux-Gendron, Jacqueline, see Ba47.

Ba51   Collette, Jean-Yves, *La Mort d'AB*, Montreal: Le Biocreux (Coll. 'Empreintes', 1), 1980, 108pp; also tr. under title *The Death of AB*, tr. Ray Chamberlain, Montreal: Guernice Editions (Prose Series, 2), 1984, 95pp.*

Ba52   Cuto, José Geraldo, *AB. A transparência do sonho*, Sao Paulo: Ed. Brasiliense, 1984.*

Ba53   *Dada/Surrealism*, 17 (1988), 'AB'. Introduction by Anna Balakian. See Bb829, 863, 872, 960, 985, 994, 1226, 1247, 1311, 1374, 1418, 1508. Includes an extensive bibliography on AB from 1972; also publ. as Anna Balakian & R. Kuentz, eds., *AB Today*, New York: Locken and Owens, 1989, 147pp.

Ba54   Durozoi, Gérard & Bernard Lecherbonnier, *AB: l'écriture surréaliste*, Paris: Larousse (Coll. 'thèmes et textes'), 1974, 255pp.

Ba55   Facioli, Valentin, *AB — Leon Trotsky. Por una arte revolucionaria independente*, Rio de Janeiro: Paz e Terra, 1985. Introduction by Gérard Roche, see Bb1388.*

Ba56   Gabellone, Lino, *L'oggetto surrealista. Il testo, la città, l'oggetto in Breton*, Turin: Einaudi (La ricerca letteraria. Serie critica, 39), 1977, 147pp.*

Ba57   Galateria, Daria, *Invito alla lettura di AB*, Milan: Mursia (Invito alla lettura. Sez. Stranieria, 13), 1977, 121pp.*

Ba58   Hozzel, Malte, *Bild und Einheitswirklichkeit im Surrealismus: Éluard und Breton*, Frankfurt, Bern & Cirencester: Lang 1980, 507pp.

Ba59   Jouanny, Robert A., *'Nadja'. André Breton. Analyse critique*, Paris: Hatier (Coll. 'Profil d'une œuvre', 36), 1972, 80pp.

Kuentz, R. & Anna Balakian, see Ba53.

Ba60   Lafitte, Maryse, *Le Surréalisme d'AB: un dépassement du politique*, Copenhagen: Romansk Institut, Københavns Universitet, 1976, 23pp.*

Ba61   Lamy, Suzanne, *AB. Hermétisme et poésie dans "Arcane 17"*, Montreal: Presses de l'Université de Montréal, 1977, 265pp.

Ba62   Lavergne, Philippe, *AB et le mythe*, Paris: Corti, 1985, 123pp.

        Lecherbonnier, Bernard, see Ba54.

Ba63   Legrand, Gérard, *AB en son temps*, Paris: Le Soleil Noir, 1976, 220pp. Contains unpubl. texts by AB [see Ac768].

Ba64   ——, *Breton*, Paris: Belfond (Coll. 'Les dossiers Belfond'), 1977, 217pp.

Ba65   Lemaître, Maurice, *Les Fautes, ignorances ou impuissances d'AB, les erreurs ou les échecs du surréalisme, reconnus par AB lui-même*, Paris: Centre de Créativité — Edit. Lettristes, 1974, unpag. [8 pp]; also in *Lettrisme* (avr.–mai–juin 79).

Ba66   *Le Magazine littéraire*, 64 (mai 72), 'AB'.   See Bb819, 840, 1112, 1180, 1425.

Ba67   *Le Magazine littéraire*, 254 (mai 88), 'AB'.   See Bb857, 897, 1000, 1022, 1091, 1181, 1249, 1319, 1358, 1400.

Ba68   Margoni, Ivos, *Per conoscere AB e il surrealismo*, Milan: Mondadori, 1976, 734pp.*

Ba69   Matthews, J.H., *AB. Sketch for an Early Portrait*, Amsterdam & Philadelphia: J. Benjamins (Purdue Univ. Monographs in Romance Langages, 22), 1986, 176pp.

Ba70   Matic, Dusan, *AB oblique*, Montpellier: Fata Morgana (Coll. 'Explorations'), 1976, 123pp. Contains Bb541; also tr. under title *AB iskosa*, tr. Miharlo Pavlovic, Belgrade: Nolit, 1979, 160pp.

Ba71   Mercurio, Vittorio, *Le Roman surréaliste: 'Nadja'. Essai d'interprétation*, Cagliari: Dattena (n.d.), 142pp.

Ba72   Mourier-Casile, Pascaline, *AB, explorateur de la Mère-Moire: trois lectures d'"Arcane 17", texte palimpseste*, Paris: PUF (Coll. 'Écrivains'), 1986, 230pp.

Ba73   Navarri, Roger, *AB: 'Nadja'*, Paris: PUF (Etudes littéraires, 11), 1986, 122pp.

Ba74   *L'Orne littéraire*, 10 (1986), 'Le Surréalisme... 20 ans après'. See Bb808, 1104, 1128, 1134, 1294, 1429, 1489.

Ba75   *Les Pharaons*, 24 (aut.75), 'AB: "Message subliminal"'. See Bb805, 883, 971, 1168, 1190.

Ba76   Pierre, José, *AB et la peinture*, Lausanne: L'Age d'Homme (Coll. 'Cahiers des avant-gardes'), 1987, 373pp.

Ba77   ——, *L'Aventure surréaliste autour d'AB*, Paris: Filipacci/Artcurial, 1986; published for exhibition, Artcurial (mai–août 86). Preface by Robert Lebel, see Bb486 (1177).

Ba78   ——, *Changer la vue. AB et la révolution surréaliste du regard* [Exhib.cat.], Centre lotois d'Arts contemporains, Musée de Cahors, 1986, 34pp.

Ba79   Pillet, Alain-Pierre, *AB à Venise*, Geneva: Iles Célèbes, 1984, 117pp.

Ba80   Plouvier, Paule, *Poétique de l'amour chez AB*, Paris: Corti, 1983, 196pp.

Ba81   Pompili, Bruno, *Breton/Aragon. Problemi del surrealismo*, Bari: Sindia, 1972, 221pp.

Ba82   Raffi, Maria Emanuela, *AB e il surrealismo nella cultura italiana (1925–1950)*, Padua: CLEUP (Letture e ricerche francesi, 1), 1986.*

Ba83   *Revue des sciences humaines*, LVI, 184 (oct.–déc.81), 'AB'. See Bb804, 987, 989, 1017, 1190, 1460.

Ba84   Robert, Bernard-Paul, *Le Surréalisme désocculté: ('Manifeste du surréalisme', 1924)*, Ottawa: Éditions de l'Université d'Ottawa, 1975, 195pp.

Bb85   Rosello, Mireille, *L'Humour noir selon AB*, Paris: Corti, 1987, 159pp.

Ba86   Rosemont, Franklin, *AB and the First Principles of Surrealism*, London: Pluto Press, 1978, 147pp.

Ba87   Saporta, Marc, ed., *AB ou le surréalisme, même*, Lausanne: L'Age d'homme (Coll. 'Mélusine'), 1988, 199pp. See Bb820, 871, 872, 916, 979, 1004, 1055, 1183, 1197, 1258, 1291, 1295, 1311, 1344, 1354, 1390, 1413, 1414, 1424, 1488.

Ba88   Schwarz, Arturo, *AB, Leone Trotsky*, Rome: Savelli, 1974*; tr. under title *AB, Trotsky et l'anarchie*, revised and enlarged edn, tr. Amaryllis Vassilikioti, Paris: UGE (Coll.10/18, 1174), 1977, 216pp. Contains Ac779, Bb748, 749, 1163.

Ba89   Sebbag, Georges, *L'Imprononçable Jour de ma naissance: 17ndré 13reton*, Paris: Jean-Michel Place, 1988, 256pp.

Ba90   Sheringham, Michael, *AB: A Bibliography*, London: Grant & Cutler (Research Bibliographies and Checklists, 2), 1972, 122pp.

Ba91   Vielwahr, André, *Sous le signe des contradictions: AB de 1913 à 1924*, Paris: Nizet, 1980, 151pp.

Ba92   Violato, Gabriella, *Scritture surrealiste*, Roma: Bulzoni (Biblioteca di cultura, 216), 1982, 192pp.

Bb93   Virmaux, Alain and Odette, *AB. Qui êtes-vous*, Lyon: La Manufacture, 1987, 158pp. Contains tributes by Blin, Brunius, Césaire, Duchamp, Estienne, Lebel, Mansour, Mascolo, Masson. Also contains Simone Collinet, 'Origines et tendances de la peinture surréaliste', extracts from a paper given in 1965–66 [unlisted].

Ba94   Vogt, Ulrich, *Le Point noir. Politik und Mythos bei AB*, Frankfurt am Main & Bern: Peter Lang, 1982, 438pp.

*b (i). Articles (including less substantial parts of books etc.) and items
published before 1972.*

Bb107a   Altman, Georges, 'Les livres. Contre la «vie» bourgeoise' [CR of *Nadja*], *L'Humanité* (3 déc.28), 4.

Bb117   To read: 'La Poésie: AB. — *Clair de terre*', *Paris-Journal*, XXXVIII, 2483 (11 jan.24), 3.

Bb118a   Aragon, Louis, 'Lautréamont et nous', *Lettres françaises* (1–7 juin, 8–15 juin 67).*

Bb118b   ——, 'Lettre ouverte à Breton sur Le Regard du sourd', *Lettres françaises*, 1388 (2 juin 71), 3, 15; also in *Œuvres poétiques croisées*, II, Paris: Livre-Club Diderot, 1974, p.26.*

Bb112a   Arland, Marcel, '*Les Pas perdus*', *La Vie des lettres*, XVI (1924), 100. [1 sentence.]

Bb134a   Audoin, Philippe, 'Lettre ouverte à Louis Aragon', *La Quinzaine littéraire*, 122 (16–31 juil.71), 8. Reply to Bb118b.

Bb148   Journal to read: *Le Centaure*, suppl. of *Gazette médicale de France*, 9 (mai 31), 4–6.

Bb182   Add: *La Critique sociale*, 1 (mars 31), 35–36; also in reprint edition, Paris: Éditions de la Différence, 1983.

Bb187a   Binni, Lanfranco, 'Un classico dell'irrazionalismo europeo. Surrealismo. Il manifesto del "24"', *Il Ponte*, XXVII, 5–6 (maggio-giugno 71), 699–718.

Bb187b   Blanche, Jacques-Emile, 'Préface du professeur AB à la *Mise sous whisky marin* du Dr Max Ernst', *Comœdia*, XV, 3068 (11 mai 21), 2. Also contains in full Ac56.

Bb188a   ——, '*Les Champs magnétiques*', *Comœdia* (7 juil.20).*

Bb201a   Bonnet, Marguerite, 'La Suite des impostures', *La Quinzaine littéraire*, 104 (16–31 oct.70), 14–15.

Bb205a   Bor, Vane, Refs in *Anti-Žid: Prilog za Pravilnije Shvacanje Nadrealizma* [Anti-Gide: Contribution to a more correct understanding of Surrealism], Belgrade: Nadrealistička Izdanja, 1932, pp.30–32, 39–41.

Bb209   Add: also in *Injustice*, Paris: La Table Ronde de Combat (Coll. 'Les Brulots'), 1969, pp.152–56.

Bb214a   Bourguet, Georges, '*Nadja*', *Le Radical* (7 juil.28).*

Bb215a   Bousquet, Joë, 'La Révolution surréaliste' [CR of *Second manifeste*], *Chantiers*, XXXVIII, 1ère série, 8 (mars 30), 26–30.

Bb215b   ——, CR of *Nadja*, *Chantiers*, 1 (jan.28), 24–27.

Bb215c   ——, '*L'Immaculée Conception*', *Carnet*, 8 (oct.31), 26–32.*

Bb230a   Bureau, Jacques, 'Lettre ouverte à AB', *Réverbères*, 1 (avr.38).*

Bb230b   Bürger, Peter, 'Valéry und Breton' (pp.51–56), 'Das *Manifeste du surréalisme*' (pp.57–75), 'Die Bedeutung des Traums im Surrealismus' (pp.87–94), 'Theorie und Praxis' (pp.96–103), 'Bretons *Nadja*' (pp.124–38), in *Der französische Surrealismus. Studien zum Problem der avantgardistischen Literatur*, Frankfurt: Athenäum, 1971.

Bb230c   ——, 'Die Dichtung Bretons', *ibid.*, pp.166–79; also in Peter Bürger, ed., *Der Surrealismus*, Darmstadt: Wissenschaftliche Buchgesellschaft, 1982, pp.231–43.

Bb240a   Carasso, E., 'Surréalisme philosophique et littéraire', *Aujourd'hui* (juil.–août 25), 6.*

Bb247a   Carrouges, Michel, 'Au seuil du hasard objectif', *Gradiva*, 2 (nov.71), 9–11.

Bb249a   Casanova, Philippe, 'Comment AB m'assassina', *L'Ame gauloise*, X, 196 (16 nov.24).*

Bb250a   Cassou, Jean, *'L'Immaculée Conception'*, *Les Nouvelles littéraires*, X, 430 (10 jan.31), 7.

Bb250b   ——, *'Point du jour'*, *Les Nouvelles littéraires*, XIII, 650 (30 mars 35), 2.

Bb259a   Charbonnier, Georges, Refs in *Entretiens avec André Masson*, Paris: Julliard (Coll. 'Lettres Nouvelles'), 1958*; new edn, Marseille: Ryôan-ji, 1985, pp.42–44, 73–76.

Bb272a   Copperie, Adrien, *'Les Pas perdus'*, *Intentions*, III, 25 (juin 24), 47–48.

Bb273a   Cranston, Mechthild, 'Breton, Éluard and Char, *Ralentir travaux*. Elective Affinities?', *Rivista di letteratura moderna e comparate*, XXIV, 2 (giugno 71), 133–50.

Bb275a   Crastre, Victor, 'Explosion surréaliste' [CR of *Manifeste du surréalisme*], *Clarté*, 74 (mai 25), 198–99.

Bb276a   ——, *'Les Pas perdus*, par AB', *Les Feuilles libres*, 36 (mars–juin 24), 403–05; also in *Mon corps et moi*, Paris: Pauvert, 1974, pp.190–92.

Bb280a   Curnier, Pierre, *'L'Amour fou* : "Tournesol"', in *Pages commentées d'auteurs contemporains*, Vol. 2, Paris: Larousse, 1965, pp.65–78.

Bb282a   Daniel-Rops, 'Au-delà de la connaissance' [CR of *Nadja*], *Signaux*, III, 2 (1 jan.29).

Bb282b   Daniel-Rops, '*Nadja*', *Chanteclerc* (8 sept.28).*

Bb285a   David, Maurice, '*Nadja*', *La Dépêche tunisienne* (17 oct.28).*

Bb286a   Decottignies, Jean, 'L'Œuvre surréaliste et l'idéologie', *Littérature*, 1 (fév.71), 30–47; also in Ba46, pp.110–16.

Bb291a   Derème, Tristan, 'Revue de fin d'année' [CR of *Manifeste du surréalisme*], *La Muse française*, 3e série, 10 (10 déc.24), 842–46.

Bb291b   Dermée, Paul, 'Autour du surréalisme' [letter to AB], *Le Journal littéraire*, 19 (30 août 24), 4.

Bb291b   ——, 'Pour en finir avec le surréalisme', *Le Mouvement accéléré* (nov.24).*

Bb303a   Dujardin, Edouard, '*Clair de terre*', *Les Cahiers idéalistes*, 11 (déc.24).*

Bb304   Add: also in Ba14.

Bb307a   Dupeyron, Georges, '*Nadja*', *Signaux*, III, 1 (1 déc.28).

Bb309   Reference to journal: *Arts*, 435 (29 oct.53), 5–6.

Bb317a   Éluard, Paul, 'AB et Philippe Soupault: *Les Champs magnétiques*', *Littérature*, 16 (sept.–oct.20), 40; also in *Œuvres complètes*, II, Paris: Gallimard (Bibl. de la Pléiade), 1968, p.773.

Bb319   Also under title 'AB est mon ami' in *Le Poète et son ombre*, Paris: Seghers, 1963, pp.51–52; also under title 'Après la confession' in *Œuvres complètes*, II [see Bb317a], pp.784–85.

Bb322a   Espiau, Marcel, 'Au pays des frères aînés', *Paris-journal* (12 jan.25).*

Bb322b   Espinosa, E., 'Navidades en primavera. Breton, Péret y Éluard, nuevos Reyes Magos en Canarias', *La Tarde* (4 mayo 35)*; also in *Textos (1927–1936)*, Santa Cruz de Tenerife: Aula de Cultura, 1980.*

Bb324a   Estienne, Charles, Ref. in 'Hommage à Antonin Artaud au Théâtre Sarah-Bernhardt', *Combat* (8 juin 46), 2. [1 paragraph on AB].

Bb335a   Fauchereau, Serge, 'Péret, Breton' [CR of Ba1, 2 paragraphs], *La Quinzaine littéraire*, 128 (1 nov.71), 15.

Bb335b   ——, CR of Ba1, *Bulletin critique du livre français*, 313 (déc.71), 1411.

Bb343a   Fontaine, '*Flagrant délit*', *Le Libertaire*, 194 (2 sept.49), 3.

Bb343b   ——, 'Sur AB', *Le Libertaire*, 224 (14 avr.50), 3.

Bb353a   Gaillard, André, 'L'Esprit et le temps' [CR of *Légitime défense*], *Les Cahiers du Sud*, XII, 85 (déc.26), 372–75.

Bb354a   Galtier-Boissière, Jean, 'A la fourchette (Le cadavre d'un surréaliste)', *Le Crapouillot* (1 mars 30), 9–10.

Bb355a   Garric, Robert, '*Manifeste du surréalisme*', *La Revue des jeunes* (25 nov.24), 430. *

Bb356a   Gauchez, Maurice, '*Les Pas perdus*', *La Renaissance d'occident* (Bruxelles), X, 3 (juin 24), 850.

Bb359a   Gauthier, Xavière, Refs in *Surréalisme et sexualité*, Paris: NRF Gallimard (Coll. 'Idées'), 1971, *passim*.

Bb362a   Gérard, Francis, '*Clair de terre*, poèmes par AB', *Philosophies*, 2 (15 mai 24), 215–16.

Bb362b   ——, 'Une Levée de boucliers' [CR of *Manifeste du surréalisme*], *La Griffe*, VI (15 jan.25), 3.

Bb362c   Germain, André, Ref. in 'Louis Aragon. *Le Libertinage*', *La Revue européenne*, II, 22 (1 déc.24), 63. Contains stinging attack on AB. [1 paragraph.]

Bb373a   Goll, Ivan, 'Autour du surréalisme' [letter to AB], *Le Journal littéraire* (30 août 24), 4.

Bb373b   Gonzague Frick, Louis de, CR of *Nadja*, *La Griffe*, IX, 27 (5 juil.28), 3.

Bb376   Reference to journal: (31 jan.48), 1. Extract from Ba17.

Bb379   Title to read: 'Spectre du *Poisson soluble*'. Also in Ba46.

Bb380a   Granell, Eugenio Fernández, interview with AB, *La Nación* (Santo Domingo) (mayo 41).*

Bb388b   Grössel, Hanns, 'Im Jahre Fünf nach Breton', *Merkur*, 282 (Okt.71), 100–06.

Bb393a   Guillaumin, Jean, 'Réel et surréel: le traitement "poétique" de la réalité dans la cure et ailleurs', *Revue française de psychiatrie*, 35 (1971), 883–919; also under title 'Rêve, réalité et surréalité dans la cure psychanalytique et ailleurs. Rêve et poésie, avec une étude sur un rêve d'AB', in *Le Rêve et le moi. Rupture, continuité, création dans la vie psychique*, Paris: PUF (Coll. 'Le fil rouge'), 1979, pp.173–209.

Bb394b   Guterman, Norbert, 'La Fin d'une histoire — quelques notes sur le "Surréalisme" dans le sens que lui donne M.Breton', *Philosophies*, 4 (15 nov.24), 445–46.

Bb396a   Habaru, Augustin, 'Populisme?' [CR of *Second manifeste*, 2 paragraphs], *Monde*, II, 81 (21 déc.29), 3.

Bb400a   Harlaire, André, *'Clair de terre'*, *Accords*, 1 (mai 24).*

Bb401   Reference to journal: (mars 24), 101–02.

Bb401a   ——, *'Les Pas perdus'*, *Accords*, 2 (juin 24).*

Bb402   Reference to journal: II, 6 (mars 29), 539–45.

Bb407   First published under title, 'Réflexions autour d'un livre: *Les Pas perdus* d'AB', *Le Disque vert*, III, 4e série (jan.25), 76–81.

Bb421a   Hubert, Renée Riese, 'André Masson and his Critics', *Comparative Literature Studies*, VII, 4 (Dec.70), 480–88.

Bb431a   Hytier, Jean, Ref. in 'Préface à l'avenir', *Le Mouton blanc*, 2e série, 3 (nov.24), 5.

Bb431b   Igert, Maurice, 'Le Surréalisme', *Les Cahiers libres*, (mai 25), 27.*

Bb432a   Ingalls, Jeremy, *'Young Cherry Trees Secured by Hares*. By AB', *Saturday Review of Literature*, XXX, 1 (4 Jan.47), 24.

Bb432b   Internationale Lettriste, 'Le "Réseau Breton" et la chasse aux rouges', *Potlatch*, 13 (23 oct.54)*; also in G. Berreby, *Documents relatifs à la fondation de l'Internationale Situationniste*, Paris: Allia, 1985, p.185.

Bb436a   Jaloux, Edmond, *'Clair de terre'*, *L'Eclair*, (11 sept.20).*

Bb438   Add: p.3.

Bb440   First published in *Marianne* (8 sept.37), 5.

Bb440a   Jarocinska, Stanislawa, '*Nadja*', *Wladomosci literackie*, 14 (avr.29).*

Bb440b   Jean, Marcel, 'L'Ukase et la romance', *Combat* (24 mai 51); also in Ac804, 105–06.

Bb461a   Julien, André, 'Le Retour d'AB', *Le Libertaire* (24 avr.47), 3.

Bb467   Author to read: Kasyade, Edouard.

Bb467a   Kemp, Robert, 'Le Surréalisme' [CR of *Manifeste du surréalisme*], *La Revue universelle*, XX, 20 (15 jan.25), 256–57.

Bb470a   ——, '*Manifeste du surréalisme*', *Le Journal littéraire*, 32 (29 nov.24), 8.

Bb476a   Lamantia, Philip, 'Surrealism in 1943' [letter to AB], *VVV*, 4 (Feb.44).*

Bb484a   Laurens, G., '*Point du jour*', *Répertoire analytique de littérature française*, II, 6 (jan.–fév.71), 63–64.*

Bb484b   Lazareff, Pierre, 'Musidora répète un sketch surréaliste', *Gringoire* (7 déc.28).*

Bb498   Add vol no: XXI, 15.

Bb503a   Le Sidaner, Louis, 'Un Roman surréaliste' [CR of *Nadja*], *La Nouvelle revue critique*, XIII, n.s., 5 (mars 29), 239.

Bb509a   López Torres, D., 'AB en Tenerife', *La Prensa* (25 apr.35).*

Bb512a   Lyotard, Jean-François, Refs in *Discours, figure*, Paris: Klincksieck, 1971 (see index).

Bb513a   Madelaigue, Jean, '*Manifeste du surréalisme*', *Le Journal du peuple*, IX, 39 (8 nov.24), 3.

Bb517a   Malespine, Emile, '*Nadja*', *L'Effort* (Lyon) (1 juin 29).*

Bb517b   M[alraux], A[ndré], '*Les Champs magnétiques*', *Action*, 5 (oct.20).*

Bb517c   Malraux, Clara, Refs in *Nos vingt ans*, Paris: Grasset, 1966.*

Bb531a   Martignon, Andrée, 'Erreurs et vérités sur le surréalisme', *Les Cahiers libres* (jan.–fév.26), 233–34.*

Bb561a   Merlin, I., 'AB et l'aventure surréaliste', in *Poètes de la révolte de Baudelaire à Michaux. Alchimie de l'être et du verbe*, Paris: l'Ecole, 1971, pp.131–53.

Bb561b   Michaux, Henri, 'Surréalisme' [CR of *Poisson soluble*], *Le Disque vert*, III, 4e série (janv.25), 82–86.

Bb569a   *Le Monde libertaire*, 126 (nov.66), 8–9. 'Témoignages', with tributes by G.-A. Bodsou, Louis Chavance, Jean Rollin and J.-C. Tertrais.

Bb574a   Morhange, Pierre, 'Lettre à A. Breton', *NRF*, XII, 134 (nov.24), 644; also extracts in *Le Journal littéraire* (18 oct.24).

Bb583a   Neuhuys, Paul, '*Les Champs magnétiques*', *Ça ira* (Anvers), 14 (1921), 60–61. [2 paragraphs.]

Bb608   Reference to journal: *NRF*, XXII, 125 (fév.24), 219–22.

Bb625a   Pfeiffer, Jean, 'AB', *Le Ciel bleu*, 6 (29 mars 45).*

Bb634a   Pierre, José, 'AB et *Combat-Art*', *Combat-Art*, 127 (9 jan.67), 2.

Bb636a   Pierre-Quint, Léon, '*Le Second Manifeste*', *La Revue de France*, XI, 20 (15 oct.31), 709–20.

Bb646a   Poulaille, Henry, '*Le Manifeste du surréalisme*', *Le Peuple*, 1437 (14 déc.24), 4.

Bb655a   Racine, Nicole, Refs in 'Une Revue d'intellectuels communistes dans les années 20: *Clarté* 1921–28', *Revue française de science politique*, XVII, 3 (juin 67).*

Bb658a   Reboux, Paul, '*Nadja*', *Chanteclerc* (1 nov.28).*

Bb670a   Richard, Elie, '*Les Pas perdus*', *Images de Paris*, V, 52 (avr.–mai 24), unpag.

Bb672a   Riffaterre, Michael, 'La Métaphore filée dans la poésie surréaliste', *Langue française*, 3 (1969), 46–60; also in *La Production du texte*, Paris: Seuil, 1979, pp.217–34.

Bb690a   Rougemont, Denis de, 'AB. *Le Manifeste du surréalisme*', *Bibliothèque universelle et Revue de Genève* (juin 25), 775–76.*

Bb700a   S., F., 'A*B. Le Manifeste du surréalisme. Poisson soluble*', *Le Divan*, XVII, 106 (fév.25), 91.

Bb703a   Saillet, Maurice, Letter to AB (23 août 46), *Néon*, 5 (1949), unpag.

Bb713a   Schwab, Raymond, '*Ralentir travaux*', *La Quinzaine critique*, II, 18 (25 juil.30), 457.

Bb713b   Scop, Celia, Refs in 'Paris Letter', *Partisan Review*, XIV, 3 (May–June 1947), 278–84 (pp.283, 284).

Bb717a   Schwarz, Arturo, Letter to AB, as preface to *The Complete Works of Marcel Duchamp*, London: Thames and Hudson, 1969, p.vii.*

Bb729a   Soupault, Philippe, '*Clair de terre*', *La Revue européenne*, II, 14 (avr.24), 54–55.

Bb739a   Testud, Pierre, '*Nadja*, ou la métamorphose', *Revue des sciences humaines*, XXXVI, 144 (oct.–déc. 71), 579–89.

Bb740a   Thomas, H., 'AB dans l'aventure humaine', *Arts*, 401 (6 mars 53), 5.

Bb744a   'Les Treize', '*Les Champs magnétiques*', *L'Intransigeant* (4 sept.20).*

Bb748   Letter dated 22 déc.1938.

Bb749a   Refs in Ungaretti, Giuseppe, *Innocence et mémoire*, tr. Philippe Jaccottet, Paris: Gallimard (Les Essais, 143), 1969, p.278.*

Bb750a   V., A., '*Les Champs magnétiques*', *Le Crapouillot* (1 sept.20).*

Bb751   Add: also in *Littérature*, 5 (juil.19), 1–5; 6 (août 19), 10–16; 7 (sept.19), 13–17; 4 letters also in Marcel Jean, *Autobiographie du surréalisme*, Paris: Seuil, 1978, pp.45–52.

Bb752a   Valmy-Baysse, Jacques, '*Les Champs magnétiques*', *Comœdia*, XIV, 2803 (19 août 20), 2.

Bb753a   Vandérem, Fernand, '*Les Champs magnétiques*', *La Revue de Paris*, XXVII, 18 (15 sept.20), 432. [1 paragraph.]

Bb753b   ——, '*Les Pas perdus*', *Revue de France*, IV, 10 (15 mai 24). [1 paragraph.]

Bb755a   Vauvrecy, A., 'Livres nouveaux: *Clair de terre*, par AB', *L'Esprit nouveau*, 21 (fév 24).

Bb763a   Refs in Waldrop, Rosemarie, *Against Language? 'Dissatisfaction with language' as Theme and as Impulse*, The Hague & Paris: Mouton, 1971.*

Bb770a   Refs in Wolff, Charlotte, *On the Way to Myself*, London: Methuen, 1969.*

Bb782a   Anon., 'Un Cadavre' [CR of *Second Manifeste*], *NRF*, XVIII, 197 (1 fév.30), 292–93.

Bb782b   ——, CR of Ba17, *Néon*, 2 (1948), unpag. [3].

Bb782c   ——, 'Un Départ', *Aux écoutes*, IX, 497 (26 nov.27), unpag. [29].

b (ii). Articles (including less substantial parts of books etc.) published between 1972 and 1989.

Bb804   Abastado, Claude, 'Écriture automatique et instance du sujet', in *Le Discours et le sujet*, Paris: Université Paris-X Nanterre, 1973, pp.202–31; also in Ba83, pp.59–75.

Bb805   ——, '"Les mots ont fini de jouer"', in Ba75, pp.17–25.

Bb806   Abel, Lionel, 'The Surrealists in New York', in *The Intellectual Follies. A Memoir of the Literary Venture in New York and Paris*, New York & London: W.W. Norton, 1984, pp.88–115; also in *Commentary*, LXXII, 4 (Oct.81), 44–54.

Bb807   Ablamowicz, Aleksander, 'La Structure du romanesque dans *Nadja* d'AB', in Jean Bessière, ed., *Signes du roman, signes de la transition*, Paris: PUF, 1986, pp.235–46.*

Bb808   Achard, Dominique, 'Émergences, hommage à AB, hiérophante du surréalisme né à Tinchebray en 1896', in Ba74, p.56.

Bb809   Adam, Jean-Michel, 'Construire le poème comme texte: lecture de "Monde" d'AB', *Pratiques*, 39 (oct.83), 29–35.

Bb810   ——, 'La métaphore productrice', in *Linguistique et discours littéraire. Théorie et pratique des textes*, Paris: Larousse (Coll. 'L'), 1976, pp.175–84.

Bb811   Adamowicz, Elza, 'Narcisse se noie: lecture de "L'Union libre" d'AB', *Romanic Review*, LXXX, 4 (Nov.89), 571–81.

Bb812   ——, 'Sortir de "la nuit du tournesol"', *La Chouette*, 3 (July 80), 14–23.

Bb813   ——, CR of Aa839, *French Studies*, XLIII, 4 (Oct.89), 488–89.

Bb814   Adamson, Ginette, 'Roussel et Breton', in *Le Procédé de Raymond Roussel*, Amsterdam: Rodopi (Coll. 'Faux titre', 15), n.d. [1984], pp.47–55.

Bb815   Albersmeier, Franz-Josef, 'Collage und Montage im surrealistischen Roman. Zu Aragons *Paysan de Paris* und Bretons *Nadja*', *Zeitschrift für Literaturwissenschaft und Linguistik*, XXI, 46 (1982), 46–63; also in *Die Herausforderung des Films an die französische Literatur. Entwurf einer Literaturgeschichte des Films*, I, 'Die Epoche des Stummfilms (1885–1930)', Heidelberg: Carl Winter Universitätsverlag, 1985, pp.351–64.*

Bb816   Albertazzi, Ferdinando, 'AB: un uomo attento', in Ba38, pp.23–34.

Bb817   Albouy, Pierre, Bb100, also in *Mythographies*, Paris: Corti, 1976, pp.47–52.

Bb818   Alexandre, Maxime, Refs in *Journal (1951–1975)*, Paris: Corti, 1976, pp.13–14, 93, 96, 120–21, 176–77, 211, 213.

Bb819   Alexandrian, Sarane, 'AB découvreur et redécouvreur d'écrivains', in Ba66, pp.16–17.

Bb820   ——, 'AB, la psychanalyse et le rêve', in Ba87, pp.154–62.

Bb821   ——, 'Breton et l'amour surréaliste', in *Les Libérateurs de l'amour*, Paris: Seuil (Coll. 'Points'), 1977, pp.207–55.

Bb822   ——, 'La Querelle des haricots', *La Quinzaine littéraire*, 204 (fév.75), 30.

Bb823   ——, 'Le Rêve dans le surréalisme', *Nouvelle revue de psychanalyse*, 5 (1972), 27–50; also in Ba46, pp.59–65.

Bb824   Alexandrian, Sarane, 'Les rêves d'AB', in *Le Surréalisme et le rêve*, Paris: Gallimard 1974, pp.241–61.

Bb825   Allan Michaud, Dominique, 'Saint-Cirq-Lapopie: dans le musée imaginaire des "Barons du Nord", la révolution surréaliste?', *NRF*, 322 (nov.79), 165–74.

Bb826   Alquié, Ferdinand, Refs in *La Conscience affective*, Paris: Vrin (Coll. 'A la recherche de la vérité'), 1979, pp.92, 97–98, 107, 170.

Bb827   ——, 'Le Surréalisme et l'art', *Études philosophiques*, 2 (avr.–juin 75), 149–59.

Bb828   Amprimoz, Alexandre L., 'Note sur l'ouverture des *Pas perdus*', *Lettres romanes*, XXXVI, 2 (mai 82), 149–56.

Bb829   Antle, Martine, 'Portrait and Anti-Portrait: From the Figural to the Spectral', in Ba53, pp.46–58.

Bb830   Antoine, Régis, 'AB et les mondes noirs', *L'Afrique littéraire*, 58 (1981), 58–70.

Bb831   ——, 'Des hommes en travers du mythe', *Mélusine*, 7 (1985), 69–86.

Bb832   Ariew, Robert, 'AB's *Poisson soluble*', *Association for Literary and Linguistic Computing Bulletin*, VI, 1 (1978), 34–41.*

Bb833   Arnaud, Noël [With Jacques Bureau, J.-Fr. Chabrun, Marc Patin], Letter to AB (14.7.43), in José Pierre, *Tracts surréalistes et déclarations collectives 1922–1969. Tome II: 1940–1969*, Paris: Losfeld/Le Terrain Vague, 1982, pp.11–17; also in Michel Fauré, *Histoire du surréalisme sous l'occupation*, Paris: La Table Ronde, 1982, pp.263–69.

Bb834   Arrouye, Jean, 'La Photographie dans *Nadja*', *Mélusine*, 4 (1983), 123–51.

Bb835   Arvidsson, Karl-Anders, 'L'Engagement politique du surréalisme', *Studia neophilologica*, LIV, 1 (1982), 149–68.

Bb836   Asari, Makoto, 'Au-delà de l'affirmation-négation. Les mythes en question: Bataille, Breton, Heidegger', *Pleine marge*, 8 (déc.88), 7–16.

Bb837   Aspley, Keith, 'AB's Poems for Denise', *French Studies*, XLI, 1 (Jan.87), 52–61.

Bb838   ——, '"La Grèce n'a jamais existé": Myth, Legend, and Ritual in the Writings of AB', in Keith Aspley, David Bellos & Peter Sharratt, eds., *Myth and Legend in French Literature. Essays in honour of A.J. Steele*, London: Modern Humanities Research Association, 1982, pp.210–26.

Bb839   Assailly, Jean, 'Psychanalystes et surréalistes, spéléologues de l'inconscient', *Le Surréalisme contestataire et contesté, Points et contrepoints*, 113 (déc.74), 18–26.

Bb840   Audoin, Philippe, 'AB: Qu'est-ce que le surréalisme?', and 'Quelques-uns des livres d'AB', in Ba66, pp.10–11 and 12–14.

Bb841   ——, Refs in *Maurice Fourré rêveur définitif suivi de Le caméléon mystique*, Paris: Le Soleil Noir, 1978 (see index).

Bb842   Auric, Georges, 'AB m'invite dans son château', in *Quand j'étais là*, Paris: Grasset, 1979, pp.125–30.

Bb843   Avni, Ora, 'Breton et l'idéologie machine à coudre-parapluie', *Littérature*, 51 (oct.83), 15–27.

Bb844   Ayer, A.J., Ref. in *Part of my Life*, London: Collins, 1977, pp.256–57.

Bb845   Baciu, Stefan, 'AB y los surrealistas en Santo Domingo' (interview with E.F. Granell), and 'AB y la "Poesía sorprendida"' (interview with Alberto Baeza Flores), in *Surrealismo latinaomericano. Preguntas y respuestas*, Cruz del Sur: Ediciones Universitarias de Valparaiso, 1979, pp.45–56 and 57–66.

Bb846   Balakian, Anna, 'AB and Psychiatry', in Enid Rhodes Peschel, Edmund D. Pellegrino, eds., *Medicine and Literature*, New York: Watson, 1980, pp.160–70.*

Bb847   ——, 'AB et l'héritage méditerranéen', in *Actes du VIe Congrès de l'Association de Littérature Comparée*, Stuttgart: Erich Bieber, 1975, pp.561–64.*

Bb848   ——, 'AB's *Les États généraux*: Revolution and Poetry', *French Review*, LXII, 6 (May 89), 1008–16.

Bb849   ——, '"Au regard des divinités", modèle poétique de Breton', *Mélusine*, 1 (1979), 215–20.

Bb850   ——, 'Breton and Drugs', *Yale French Studies*, 50 (Apr.74), 96–107.

Bb851   ——, 'Breton in the light of Apollinaire', in Mary Ann Caws, ed., *About French Poetry from Dada to 'Tel Quel'. Text and Theory*, Detroit: Wayne State U.P., 1974, pp.42–53.

Bb852   ——, 'Fragments on Reality by Baudelaire and Breton', *New York Literary Forum*, 8–9 (1981), 101–09.

Bb853   Balakian, Anna, 'From Mallarmé to Breton: Continuity and Discontinuity in the Poetics of Ambiguity', in Mary Ann Caws, ed., *Writing in a Modern Temper, Essays on French Literature and Thought in Honor of Henri Peyre*, Saratoga, California: Anma Libri, 1984, pp.117–35.

Bb854   ——, 'From *Poisson soluble* to *Constellations*: Breton's Trajectory for Surrealism', *Essays on Surrealism, Twentieth Century Literature*, XXI, 1 (Feb.75), 48–58; also tr. under title 'La Trajectoire poétique d'AB: de *Poisson soluble* à *Constellations*', in Maurice Cagnon, ed., *Éthique et esthétique dans la littérature française du XXe siècle*, Saratoga, California: Anma Libri, 1978, pp.69–77.

Bb855   Balibar, Renée, 'Du Surréalisme aux comptines', in *Les Français fictifs*, Paris: Hachette, 1974, pp.220–23.

Bb856   Bancquart, Marie-Claire, 'Lecture d'*Arcane 17*', in Daniel Bougnoux and Jean-Charles Gateau, eds., *Le Surréalisme dans le texte*, Grenoble: Publications de l'Université des Langues et Lettres de Grenoble, 1978, pp.281–92.

Bb857   ——, 'Paris, capitale du désir', in Ba67, pp.36–38.

Bb858   ——, 'Surréalisme et "génie du lieu": AB', *Permanence du surréalisme, Les Cahiers du XXe siècle*, 4 (1975), 79–95.

Bb859   Baron, Pierre, 'De Freud à Breton: entre la proie et l'ombre. Quelques aspects d'un héritage', *Champs des activités surréalistes*, 19 (déc.83), 24–135.

Bb860   Baude, Jean-Marie, 'Culpabilité et valeurs morales chez AB', *Mélusine*, 8 (1986), 19–36.

Bb861   ——, 'Surréalisme et psychanalyse: sublimation', *Le Texte et son double, Le Siècle éclaté*, 3 (1985), 5–19.

Bb862   Beauge-Rosier, Jacqueline, 'Transfert du mythe dans *Nadja*', *Conjonction* (1987), 136–62.*

Bb863   Beaujour, Michel, 'Breton's *Ode à Charles Fourier* and the Poetics of Genre', in Ba53, pp.121–28.

Bb864   ——, 'La Poétique de l'automatisme chez AB', *Poétique*, 25 (1976), 116–23.

Bb865   ——, 'Transparence et opacité dans la poésie d'AB', *Mélusine*, 2 (1981), 117–29.

Bb866   Beauvoir, Simone de, Bb170, tr. under title 'Breton and Poetry', tr. H.M.Parshley, in *The Second Sex*, Harmondsworth: Penguin, 1972, pp.261–68.

Bb867   Bédouin, Jean-Louis, Letter to AB (1967), in Ba38, pp.147–55.

Bb868   ——, 'Le Surréalisme après AB', *Les Nouvelles littéraires*, LII, 2445 (5–11 aout 74), 8–9.

Bb869   Béhar, Henri, Bb174, also in *Le Théâtre dada et surréaliste*, revised edition, Paris: Gallimard (Coll. 'Idées'), 1979, pp.233–55.

Bb870   ——, 'Hermétisme, pataphysique et surréalisme', in Anna Balakian, J.James, Douwe W.Fokkema, eds., *Proceedings of the Xth Congress of the International Comparative Literature Association*, New York: Garland, 1985, pp.495–504.*

Bb871   ——, 'Repères chronologiques', in Ba87, pp.193–97.

Bb872   ——, 'The Passionate Attraction: AB and the Theatre', in Ba53, pp.13–18; also in French, under title 'L'Attraction passionnelle du théâtre', in Ba87, pp.76–86.

Bb873   Béhar, Henri, 'Zinzolin', in *Littéruptures*, Lausanne: L'Age d'homme (Bibl.Mélusine), 1988, pp.257-60 and *passim* (see index).

Bb874   Bellemin-Noël, Jean, 'AB: des vases trop communicants', in *Biographies du désir*, Paris: PUF (Coll. 'Écriture'), 1988, pp.123-208.

Bb875   Benamou, Michel, 'Surrealist Writing: Metallic Feathers on a Soluble Fish', *Teaching Language Through Literature*, XVII, 1 (1977), 1-14.*

Bb876   Bénédite, Daniel, Refs in *La Filière marseillaise: un chemin vers la liberté sous l'occupation*, Paris: Clancier Guénaud (Coll. 'Mémoire pour demain'), 1984, pp.116-18, 120-22, 124-25, 148, 211-17.

Bb877   Berranger, Marie-Paule, Refs in *Dépaysement de l'aphorisme*, Paris: Corti, 1988 (see index).

Bb878   ——, 'Paul Valéry corrigé par AB et Paul Éluard. Notes', *Pleine marge*, 1 (1985), 88-96.

Bb879   Bersani, Jacques, 'Le Champ du désespoir: essai d'analyse de "La Glace sans tain"', in *Le Surréalisme dans le texte* [see Bb856], pp.19-31.

Bb880   Berthet, Frédéric. 'Éléments de conversation: "métacommuniquer"', *Communications*, 30 (1979), 118-20.

Bb881   Bertozzi, G. A., Refs in *Rimbaud attraverso i movimenti d'avanguardia*, Rome: Luciano Lucarini, 1976, pp.82-84, 102-03, 108.

Bb882   Bertrand, Marc, 'Nadja: un secret de fabrication surréaliste', *L'Information littéraire*, XXI, 2 (mars–avr.79), 82–90, and 3 (mai–juin 79), 125–30.

Bb883   Biès, Jean, 'AB et le "point suprême"', in Ba75, pp.36–46.

Bb884   Bigongiari, Piero, 'La congiuntura Ungaretti-Breton-Reverdy', *Approdo letterario* (Florence), XVIII, 59–60 (sett.–dic.72), 31–43.

Bb885   Bimonte, Ada, 'Breton e Artaud', in *Alle fonti dell'avanguardia: da Alfred Jarry a Arthur Adamov*, Rome: La Navicella, 1979, pp.107–32.

Bb886   Binni, Lanfranco, 'AB', in *Quattro studi francesi: Lesage, Diderot, Zola, Breton*, Rome: Bulzoni, 1979, pp.101–22.

Bb887   Bishop, Michael, 'Image, *justesse*, and Love: Breton, Reverdy, and Bonnefoy', *Symposium*, XLII, 3 (Fall 88), 187–97.

Bb888   Blachère, Jean-Claude, 'Géographie physique et poétique de l'Éden chez AB', *Mélusine*, 7 (1985), 100–17.

Bb889   Boatto, Alberto, 'Sull'erotismo: Sade, Bataille, Breton', in Filiberto Menna, ed., *Studi sul surrealismo*, Rome: Officina Edizioni, 1976, pp.97–103.

Bb890   Bohn, Willard, 'At the Crossroads of Surrealism: Apollinaire and Breton', *Kentucky Romance Quarterly*, XXVII, 1 (1980), 85–96.

Bb891   ——, 'L'Image surréaliste', *Mélusine*, 2 (1981), 211–21.

Bb892   ——, 'Semiosis and Intertextuality in Breton's "Femme et oiseau"', *Romanic Review*, LXXVI, 4 (Nov.85), 415–28.

Bb893   Bohn, Willard, 'From Surrealism to surrealism: Apollinaire and Breton', *Journal of Aesthetics and Art Criticism*, XXXVI, 2 (Winter 77), 197–210.

Bb894   Boissier, Gilbert, 'Insignifiance et sursignifiance: lecture des *Champs magnétiques*', in *Le Génie et la forme. Mélanges de langue et de littérature offerts à Jean Mourot*, Nancy: Presses Universitaires de Nancy, 1982, pp.577–87.

Bb895   Bonnefoy, Claude, 'L'écriture libérée, Breton', in *Écrivains illustres*, Paris: Hachette, 1972.*

Bb896   Bonnet, Marguerite, Refs in *L'Affaire Barrès*, Paris: Corti (Coll. 'Actual'), *passim*.

Bb897   ——, 'AB le tamanoir', in Ba67, pp.39–40.

Bb898   ——, 'AB: Naissance de l'aventure surréaliste', *L'Information littéraire*, XXVI, 5 (nov.–déc.75), 213–16.

Bb899   ——, 'Entre le nihilisme et la poésie. Le chemin d'AB' (interview by François Bott), *Le Monde [des livres]*, 9387 (21 mars 75), 19.

Bb900   ——, 'A partir de ces "mécaniques à la fois naïves et véhémentes..."', *Pleine marge*, 1 (mai 85), 18–28.

Bb901   ——, 'A propos de "L'Introduction au discours sur le peu de réalité"', in *Le Surréalisme dans le texte* [see Bb856], pp.115–24.

Bb902   ——, CR of Ba62, *Revue d'histoire littéraire de la France*, 80, 1 (jan.–fév.80), 149–50.

Bb903   ——, Bb204, also in *Cahiers Léon Trotsky*, 25 (mars 86), 5–17.

Bb904   Bonnet, Marguerite & Étienne-Alain Hubert, 'Sur deux types d'écriture surréaliste et leurs finalités dans *L'Immaculée Conception* d'AB et Paul Éluard', *Revue d'histoire littéraire de la France*, LXXXVII, 4 (juil.–août 87), 753–58.

Bb905   Bott, François, 'Les Amazonies de l'inconscient', 'Octobre 24 — *Le Manifeste du Surréalisme*', *Le Monde [des livres]*, 9256 (18 oct.74), 18.

Bb906   Boulestreau, Nicole, 'L'Épreuve de la nomination dans le premier *Manifeste du surréalisme*', *Littérature*, 39 (oct.80), 47–53.

Bb907   ——, '*Nadja* d'AB: entre le livre du désir et le désir du livre', *Livre et littérature: dynamisme d'un archétype*, *Littérales* (Paris X — Nanterre), 1 (1986), 95–108.

Bb908   Bourassa, André Gilles, Refs in *Surréalisme et littérature québécoise*, Montréal: Étincelle, 1977; also tr. under title *Surrealism and Quebec Literature. History of a Cultural Revolution*, Toronto, Buffalo & London: Univ. of Toronto Press, 1984 (see index).

Bb909   Bourdil, Pierre-Yves, 'Le Merveilleux et le quotidien (lecture de *Nadja*)', *Cahiers philosophiques*, 28 (sept.86), 57–77; also in *Les Miroirs du moi. Les héros et les fous*, Paris: Édn de l'École, 1987, pp.109–26.

Bb910   Bourin, André, 'Un terroriste au Panthéon' [CR of Aa839], *Revue des deux mondes*, 9 (sept.88), 213–17.

Bb911   Bowie, Malcolm, CR of Ba8, *French Studies*, XXIX, 2 (Apr.75), 235–36.

Bb912   ——, CR of Ba90, *ibid.*, XXIX, 3 (July 75), 353.

Bb913   Brandt, Per Aage, 'The White-Haired Generator', *Poetics*, 6 (1972), 72–83.

Bb914   Brasseur, Pierre, Refs in *Ma vie en vrac*, Paris: Calmann-Lévy, 1972, pp.127–29.

Bb915   Brau, Jean-Louis, 'Les Obsèques d'AB', *Le Figaro littéraire* (18 nov.72), 15.

Bb916   Brémondy, Gisèle, 'La grande promesse', in Ba87, pp.135–40.

Bb917   Bridel, Yves, Refs in *Miroirs du surréalisme*, Lausanne: L'Age d'Homme (Coll. 'Bibliothèque Mélusine'), 1988.

Bb918   Brincourt, André, 'AB devant son paradoxe' [CR of Aa839], *Le Figaro littéraire* (27 juin 88), 32.

Bb919   ——, 'Il y a dix ans, AB', *ibid.* (16–17 oct.76), 15.

Bb920   Briosi, Sandro, 'Le "Paradoxe" de la littérature et sa "solution" dans l'avant-garde', in Sandro Briosi & Henk Hillenaar, eds., *Vitalité et contradictions de l'avant-garde. Italie-France 1909–1924*, Paris: Corti, 1988, pp.51–58.

Bb921   Broustra, Jean, 'Osiris est un dieu noir', *L'Évolution psychiatrique*, XLIV, 1 (jan.–mars 79), 59–77.

Bb922   Brown, Frederick, 'Creation versus Literature: Breton and the Surrealist Movement', in John K.Simon, ed., *Modern French Criticism. From Proust and Valéry to Structuralism*, Chicago, London: Univ. of Chicago Press, 1972, pp.123–47.*

Bb923   Brugnolo, Stefano, 'AB e la psicoanalisi: un incontro mancato?', *Studi francesi*, XXXII, 96, fasc.III (sett.–dic.88), 437–57.

Bb924   Brun, Marcel, Ref. in *Les Techniques de la poésie libre*, Albi: Impr. Coopérative du Sud-Ouest, 1978, pp.53–61.

Bb925   Brunetière, Hervé, 'Quelques remarques sur *Nadja*, de Breton', *L'Évolution psychiatrique*, LI, 1 (jan.–mars 86), 119–25.

Bb926   Bruno, Jean, 'AB et l'expérience de l'illumination', *Mélusine*, 2 (1981), 53–69.

         Bureau, Jacques, see Bb833.

Bb927   Bürger, Peter, 'Valéry und Breton. Zwei Lesarten der Moderne', *Neue Rundschau*, XCVI, 2 (1985), 31–57.

Bb928   Busi, Frederick, 'Hegel and the Origins of Surrealism and the New Left', *Contemporary French Civilization*, II, 3 (Spring 78), 379–403.

Bb929   Butor, Michel & Michel Launay, 'Breton ou la grève des signes', in *Résistances. Conversations aux Antipodes*, Paris: PUF (Coll. 'Écriture'), 1983, pp.131–34.

Bb930   Cacciavillani, Giovanni, 'Breton: l'ordine del discorso e la cattura dell'inconscio', in *Il Corpo testuale. Saggi e ricerche sulla letteratura francese*, Abano Terme: Francisci, 1982, pp.143–59.

Bb931   ——, 'Teoria e pratiche testuali del surrealismo', *Strumenti critici*, VIII, 25, fasc.III (ott.74), 306–22.

Bb932   Caillois, Roger, 'Lettre à AB' (27 déc.34), *Les Nouvelles littéraires*, LII, 2445 (5–11 août 74), 10; also in *Approches de l'imaginaire*, Paris: Gallimard, 1974, pp.35–38.

Bb933   ——, Refs in *La Nécessité d'esprit*, Paris: Gallimard, 1981, pp.88–89, 94, 169–70.

Bb934 Caillois, Roger, 'La querelle des "Haricots sauteurs"', in *Rencontres*, Paris: PUF (Coll. 'Écriture'), 1978, pp.290–94.

Bb935 Calas, Nicolas, 'Freedom, Love and Poetry', *Art Forum*, 22, 9 (May 78), 22–27.*

Bb936 Calheiros, Pedro, 'Marxisme et surréalisme dans *Les Vases communicants*', *Interférences*, 7 (jan.–juin 78), 49–75.*

Bb937 Camfield, William, Refs in *Francis Picabia. His Art, Life and Times*, Princeton, N.J.: Princeton U.P., 1979 (see index).

Bb938 Caminade, Pierre, 'Le *Manifeste du surréalisme* (1924). AB et Pierre Reverdy', and 'Du *Manifeste du surréalisme* (1924) à *La Clé des champs* (1953)', in *Image et métaphore. Un problème de poétique contemporaine*, Paris: Bordas (Coll. 'Études supérieures'), 1970, pp.26–33, and 51–53.

Bb939 Carassou, Michel, Refs in 'Les Lettres de guerre de Jacques Vaché', in *Jacques Vaché et le groupe de Nantes*, Paris: Jean-Michel Place, 1986, pp.237–52.

Bb940 Cardinal, Roger, 'Nadja and Breton', *University of Toronto Quarterly*, XLI, 3 (Spring 72), 183–99.

Bb941 ——, 'The Political Resonances of *Nadja*', *La Chouette*, 22 (July 89), 39–52.

Bb942 ——, 'The Quest for Surrealism' [CR of Ba45], *TLS*, 3869 (7 May 76), 548.

Bb943 ——, 'Savage and Civilized' [CR of At947], *TLS*, 4230 (27 Apr.84), 450.

Bb944 ——, 'Surrealist Beauty', *Forum for Modern Language Studies*, IX, 4 (Oct.74), 348–56.

Bb945   Cardinal, Roger, CR of Ba4, *French Studies*, XXVIII, 2 (Apr.74), 229–30.

Bb946   ——, CR of Ba61, 73 and 80, *French Studies*, XLII, 1 (Jan.88), 108–10.

Bb947   ——, CR of At957, *Queens Quarterly*, XCI, 4 (Winter 84), 1029–31.

Bb948   Carlino, M., '*Nadja* o delle povertà scrittoria del surrealismo', *Annali dell'Istituto di Filologia Moderna*, Rome: Editer, 1977, pp.175–87.*

Bb949   Carrington, Leonora, Letter to AB (20 août 59), in Aa606; also in Erika Billeter and José Pierre, eds., *La Femme et le surréalisme*, Lausanne: Musée Cantonal des Beaux-Arts, 1987, p.489 [Exhib.cat.].

Bb950   Carrouges, Michel, 'La Dynamique de l'occultation', *Mélusine*, 2 (1981), 39–52.

Bb951   Cassanyes, M., 'Sobre l'exposiciò Picabia i la conferéncia de Breton', in *Francis Picabia*, Barcelona: Ministerio de Cultura, 1985 [Exhib.cat.].*

Bb952   Castoldi, Alberto, Refs in *Intellettuali e fronte popolare in Francia*, Bari: De Donato, 1978.*

Bb953   Cau, Jean, Ref. in *Croquis de mémoire*, Paris: Julliard, 1985, p.172.

Bb954   Cauvin, Jean-Pierre, CR of Ba93, *French Review*, LV, 4 (March 82), 557–58.

Bb955   ——, 'Literary Games of Chance: the AB Manuscripts', *Library Chronicle of the University of Texas*, 16 (1981), 16–41.*

Bb956   Cauvin, Jean-Pierre, 'The Poethics of AB', as introduction to At955, pp.xvii-xxxviii.

Bb957   Caws, Mary Ann, 'Vers une architexture du poème surréaliste', in *Éthique et esthétique*...[see Bb854], pp.59-68.

Bb958   ——, CR of Ba1 and Ba12, *French Review*, XLVI, 2 (Dec.72), 422-23.

Bb959   ——, Refs in *The Eye in the Text. Essays on Perception, Mannerist to Modern*, Princeton, New Jersey: Princeton U.P., 1981 (see index).

Bb960   ——, 'Linkings and Reflections: AB and His Communicating Vessels', in Ba53, pp.91-100.

Bb961   ——, 'The Meaning of Surrealism, and Why it Matters', in *Writing in a Modern Temper* [see Bb853], pp.146-63.

Bb962   ——, 'Notes on a Manifesto Style: 1924 Fifty Years later', *JGE Journal of General Education* (PA), 27 (1975), 88-90.*

Bb963   ——, 'The Poetics of a Surrealist Passage and Beyond', *Twentieth Century Literature*, XXI, 1 (Feb.75), 24-36; revised version in *A Metapoetics of the Passage. Architextures in Surrealism and After*, Hanover & London: U.P. of New England, 1981, pp.27-35.

Bb964   Cazals, Patrick, Ref. in *Musidora la dixième muse*, Paris: Henri Veyrier, 1978, pp.64-68.

Bb965   Celli, Giorgio, 'La creazione non è finita', in Ba38, pp.35-43.

Bb966   Cellier, Léon, 'Breton et Nerval', *Permanence du surréalisme, Les Cahiers du XXe Siècle*, 4 (1975), 49–64; also in *Parcours initiatiques*, Neuchâtel: La Baconnière (Coll. 'Langages'), Grenoble: Presses Universitaires de Grenoble, 1977, pp.288–300.

Bb967   Cesbron, Georges, CR of Ba1, *Impacts*, n.s., 1 (1973), 102–05.

Bb968   ——, CR of Ba1, *Lettres romanes*, XXVII, 2 (mai 73), 197–203.

Chabrun, J.-Fr., see Bb833.

Bb969   Champigny, Robert, 'The First Person in *Nadja*', in *About French Poetry...* [see Bb851], pp.242–53.

Bb970   ——, 'The S Device', *Dada/Surrealism*, 1 (1971), 3–7.

Bb971   Chantrell, Lydie, 'Les Étoiles', in Ba75, pp.13–16.

Bb972   Chapelan, Maurice, '"Pape"? Non: "Antipère"'[CR of Ba56], *Le Figaro littéraire*, 1498, (1 fév.75), 15.

Bb973   Chapon, François, 'La Bibliothèque littéraire de Jacques Doucet', *Bulletin du bibliophile*, 1 (1980), 68–81.

Bb974   ——, 'Mes jeunes tigres...', in *Mystères et splendeurs de Jacques Doucet*, Paris: Lattès, 1984, pp.261–307. Includes extracts from letters written by AB to Doucet.

Bb975   Chatard, Jean, 'AB aux États-Unis', *Le Domaine poétique international du surréalisme, Le Puits de l'ermite* (Chantilly), 29–30–31 (mars 78), 89–90.

Bb976   Chénieux-Gendron, Jacqueline, 'AB: "Introduction au discours sur le peu de réalité"', in *Le Surréalisme dans le texte* [see Bb856], pp.129–45.

Bb977   Chénieux-Gendron, Jacqueline, 'Bavardage et merveille. Repenser le surréalisme', *Nouvelle revue de psychanalyse*, XL (aut.89), 273–86.

Bb978   ——, 'Breton, Leiris: l'espace forcené', in Jean-Michel Collot & Jean-Claude Mathieu, eds., *Espace et poésie*, Paris: Presses de l'École Normale Supérieure, 1987, pp.149–58.

Bb979   ——, 'L'Expérience vive du récit dans le surréalisme', in Ba87, pp.66–75.

Bb980   ——, 'Lectures surréalistes du roman noir', *Europe*, LXII, 659 (mars 84), 133–46.

Bb981   ——, 'Plaisir(s) de l'image', in *Du surréalisme et du plaisir*, Paris: Corti, 1986, pp.85–97.

Bb982   ——, 'La Position du sujet chez Breton et Bataille', in Jacqueline Chénieux-Gendron & Marie-Claire Dumas, eds., *L'Objet au défi*, Paris: PUF (Coll. 'Champs des activités surréalistes'), 1987, pp.59–76.

Bb983   ——, 'Pour une imagination pratique. AB :"Il y aura une fois..."', *L'Information littéraire*, XXIV, 5 (nov.–déc.72), 230–06; also in Ba46, pp.83–97.

Bb984   ——, 'Les Risques du dialogue: Jacques Rivière et les surréalistes', *Revue d'histoire littéraire de la France*, LXXXVII, 5 (sept.–oct.83), 884–900.

Bb985   ——, 'Towards a New Definition of Automatism: *L'Immaculée conception*', in Ba53, pp.74–90.

Bb986   ——, 'Les Variantes de *Nadja* (1928–1963): une nouvelle *version* du texte?', *Seminari pasquali di bagni di Lucca* (Pisa), 3 (1989), 5–18.

Bb987   Chénieux-Gendron, Jacqueline, 'Versants et versions du surréalisme français', in Ba83, pp.11-31.

Bb988   Cheymol, Pierre, 'AB poète', in *Les Aventures de la poésie*, Vol. II, Paris: Corti, 1988, pp.223-30.

Bb989   Clébert, Jean-Paul, 'Traces de Nadja', in Ba83, pp.79-94.

Bb990   Clej, Alina, 'Phantoms of the *opera* : Notes Towards a Theory of Surrealist Confession — The Case of Breton', *Modern Language Notes*, CIV, 4 (Sept.89), 819-44.

Bb991   Clémentin, Jean, 'A l'écoute de l'homme pour en extraire l'or du temps' [CR of Aa839], *Le Canard enchaîné* (24 août 88), 7.

Bb992   Coetzee, J.M., 'Surreal Metaphors and Random Processes', *Journal of Literary Semiotics* (Kent), VIII, 1 (1979), 22-30.

Bb993   Cohen, Jean, 'Poétique du surréalisme', in *Vitalité et contradictions...*[see Bb920], pp.77-84.

Bb994   Cohen, Margaret, 'Mysteries of Paris: The Collective Uncanny in AB's *Amour fou*', in Ba53, pp.101-10.

Bb995   Collier, Peter, 'Dreams of a revolutionary culture: Gramsci, Trotsky and Breton', in Peter Collier & Edward Timms, eds., *Vision and Blueprints: Avant-Garde Culture and Radical Politics in Early Twentieth-Century Europe*, Manchester: Manchester U.P., 1988, pp.33-51.

Bb996   ——, 'Surrealist city narrative: Breton and Aragon', in David Kelley & Edward Timms, eds., *Unreal City: Urban Experience in Modern European Literature and Art*, New York: St. Martin's Press, 1985, pp.214-29.

Bb997   Cornec, Gilles, Refs in 'Les Bonnes Fées d'Arthur Rimbaud II', *Infini*, 9 (hiver 85), 86–109.

Bb998   Cornille, Jean-Louis, '"Béthune! Béthune!"', in *Vitalité et contradictions*...[see Bb920], pp.149–58.

Bb999   Cortanze, Gérard de, 'Breton du côté de Guermantes', *Le Magazine littéraire*, 246 (oct.87), 39.

Bb1000   ——, 'L'Œuvre critique', in Ba67, pp.43–46.

Bb1001   Corti, José, Refs in *Souvenirs désordonnés*, Paris: Corti, 1983, pp.117–43.

Bb1002   Costa, Corrado, 'Gli occhi di Isis', in Ba38, pp.44–50.

Bb1003   Cottenet-Hage, Madeleine, 'Magnetic Fields II: From Breton to Duras', *French Review*, LVIII, 4 (March 85), 540–50.

Bb1004   Courtot, Claude, 'Le Mercure et le soufre', in Ba87, pp.56–65.

Bb1005   Cowling, Elizabeth, '"Proudly we claim him as one of us": Breton, Picasso and the Surrealist Movement', *Art History*, VIII, 1 (March 85), 82–104.

Bb1006   Crevel, René, 'Brouillon de lettre à un dirigeant communiste (6 juil.33)', in *Les Pieds dans le plat*, Paris: Pauvert, 1974, pp.293–94.

Bb1007   Cruz-Ramirez, Alfredo, 'Au Mexique', in *La Planète affolée. Surréalisme dispersion et influences 1938–1947*, Paris: Flammarion, Marseille: Dir. des Musées de Marseille, 1986, pp.91–96 [Exhib.cat.].

Bb1008   Curtis, Jean-Louis, Refs in *Questions à la littérature*, Paris: Stock, 1973, pp.50–51, 60, 65–70, 87.

Bb1009   Dachy, Marc, 'AB et Philippe Soupault: *Le Manuscrit des "Champs magnétiques"*', *Le Magazine littéraire*, 213 (déc.84), 31.

Bb1010   Dahmer, Helmut, 'Versäumte Lektionen Aufsätze von AB in deutscher Übersetzung', *Psyche*, XXXVI (1983).*

Bb1011   Dali, Salvador, 'Quelles étaient les divergences entre Breton, le mouvement et Dali?', *Comment on devient Dali*, Paris: Laffont, 1973, pp.144–45.*

Bb1012   Daix, Pierre, Refs in *Aragon: une vie à changer*, Paris: Seuil, 1975, *passim*.

Bb1013   Danier, Richard, 'AB et l'hermétisme alchimique', *Question de*, XV, 1 (nov.–déc.76), 47–57.

Bb1014   Daumal, René, Bb284 and 285 in *Le Grand Jeu* [facsimile reprint], Paris: Jean-Michel Place, 1972.

Bb1015   Davoine, J.-P., 'Calembour surréaliste et calembour publicitaire', *Studi francesi*, XIX, 57, fasc.III (sett.–dic.75), 481–87.

Bb1016   Décaudin, Michel, 'Autour du premier Manifeste', in P.A.Jannini, ed., *Surréalisme-surrealismo*, Rome: Bulzoni (Quaderni del novecento francese, 2), Paris: Nizet, 1974, pp.27–47.

Bb1017   Decottignies, Jean, 'Le Poète et la statue', in Ba83, pp.95–117.

Bb1018   Deguy, Michel, 'Le Demain joueur' [CR of Aa484], *Les Cahiers du chemin*, 19 (15 oct.73), 103–10.

Bb1019   ——, 'Du "Signe ascendant" au "Sphinx vertébral"', *Poétique*, 34 (avr.78), 226–40.

Bb1020   De Haes, Frans, '"Inflation verbale", surréalisme. Tel Quel, Lautréamont', *Lautréamont, Entretiens*, 30 (1971), 186–93.

Bb1021   Deltel, Danielle, 'Visions et imagination dans *Arcane 17* d'AB: une transmutation éblouissante', *Annales de la Faculté des Lettres et Sciences Humaines de Yaoundé*, IX (1979), 103–17.

Bb1022   Delvaille, Bernard, 'De la modernité du symbolisme', in Ba67, pp.30–31.

Bb1023   Demangeat, Michel, 'Freud, Breton, Lacan: un sentier forestier', in *Surréalisme*, *Eidolon* (Université de Bordeaux III), 21 (mai 82), 53–75.

Bb1024   Demers, Jeanne, & Line MacMurray, Refs in *L'Enjeu du manifeste/Le manifeste en jeu*, Longueuil (Quebec): Le Préambule, 1986.*

Bb1025   Desnos, Robert, 'AB', and 'La Fin de Dada. La Rupture avec AB', in Marie-Claire Dumas, ed., *Nouvelles Hébrides et autres textes, 1922–1930*, Paris: Gallimard, 1978, pp.296–300 and 328–39. Also contains Bb295 and 296.

Bb1026   ——, Letter to AB (4 avr.23), in Marie-Claire Dumas, ed., *Robert Desnos*, *Les Cahiers de l'Herne*, Paris: Herne, 1987, 287–88.

Bb1027   Dhainault, Pierre, 'L'Éclair noir, la lumière blanche', *Gradiva*, 3, (1972), 2–5.

Bb1028   Dhoeve, Andries, 'Greppels om een siepelbed', *Nieuw Vlaams Tijdschrift* (Antwerp), 28 (1975), 950–95.*

Bb1029   Dollé, Jean-Paul, 'Breton et Freud', *Le Magazine littéraire*, 213 (déc.84), 35.

Bb1030   Drachline, Pierre, 'Les Ages d'or. Défense et illustration de la personne et de l'œuvre d'AB', *Le Monde [des livres]*, 13470 (20 mai 88), 22.

Bb1031   Drijkoningen, Fernand F.J., 'Comment lire un poème-objet', in Raimund Theis & Hans T. Siepe, eds., *Le Plaisir de l'intertexte: formes et fonctions de l'intertextualité*, Frankfurt, Bonn & New York: Peter Lang, 1986, pp.91–110.

Bb1032   ——, 'De Nacht van de heliotroop: Een surrealistisch model van lezen en interpreteren', *Forum der Letteren* (Leyden), XX, 3 (sept.79), 159–67 (353–61).

Bb1033   Dunaway, John M., 'Maritain and Breton: Common Denominators in the Aesthetic Confrontation of Thomism and Surrealism', *Authors and Philosophers, French Literature Series* (Columbia), 6 (1979), 16–25.

Bb1034   Durand, Pascal, 'Pour une lecture institutionnelle du *Manifeste du surréalisme*', *Mélusine*, 8 (1986), 177–95.

Bb1035   Durozoi, Gérard, 'Breton, Péret et quelques autres', in Jean-Michel Goutier, ed., *Benjamin Péret*, Paris: Henri Veyrier, 1982, pp.33–47.

Bb1036   ——, 'Notes sur la métaphore poétique et la métaphore picturale dans le surréalisme', *Les Cahiers du XXe siècle*, 4 (1975), 109–21; also in *Horizon*, XVIII, 1 (Winter 76), 109–21.*

Bb1037   Eberz, Ingrid, 'Kandinsky, Breton et le modèle purement intérieur', *Pleine marge*, 1 (1985), 69–80.

Bb1038   Edelman, Jan, 'Les Associations en liberté', *Rapports — Het Franse Boek*, LI, 2 (1981), 49–58.

Bb1039   Eigeldinger, Marc, 'AB et la lecture de Huysmans', in Pierre
          Brunel & André Guyaux, eds., *Huysmans, Les Cahiers de
          l'Herne*, Paris: l'Herne, 1985, pp.436–45; also in *Mythologie et
          intertextualité*, Geneva: Slatkine, 1987, pp.157–69.*

Bb1040   ——, 'AB et le mythe de l'âge d'or', *Mélusine*, 7 (1985), 17–32.

Bb1041   ——, 'AB et l'expérience de la liberté', and 'La Mythologie du
          papillon chez AB', in *Poésie et métamorphoses*, Neuchâtel: La
          Baconnière, 1973, pp.183–202 and 203–18. Also contains Bb313.

Bb1042   ——, 'AB révélateur de Germain Nouveau', *Studi francesi*,
          XXV, 73, fasc.I (genn.–apr.81), 37–45.

Bb1043   ——, 'Celtisme et surréalisme', in Peter Bürger, ed., *Der
          Surrealismus*, Darmstadt: Wissenschaftliche Buchgesellschaft,
          1982, pp.411–17.

Bb1044   ——, 'Poésie et langage alchimique chez AB', *Mélusine*, 2
          (1981) 22–38; also in *Lumières du mythe*, PUF (Coll. 'Écriture'),
          1983, pp.175–96.

Bb1045   ——, 'Structures mythiques d'*Arcane 17*', *ibid.*, pp.197–220.

Bb1046   Encrenaz, Olivier & Jean Richer, *Vivante étoile. Michel-Ange,
          Gérard de Nerval, AB*, Paris: Lettres Modernes (Archives des
          Lettres Modernes, 8, Archives nervaliennes, 9), 1971 (8) (VII),
          127[460-6].

Bb1047   Erickson, John D., 'Surrealist Black Humor as Oppositional
          Discourse', *Symposium*, XLII, 3 (Fall 88), 198–215.

Bb1048   Esteban, Claude, 'Un Lieu hors de tout lieu (II)', *Argile*, XVI
          (été 78), 92–105; also in *Un Lieu hors de tout lieu*, Paris:
          Galilée, 1979, pp.77–91.

Bb1049   Fauchereau, Serge, 'Des questions pour aujourd'hui', *Digraphe*, 30 (juin 83), 18–23.

Bb1050   Fauskevag, Svein Eirik, Refs in *Sade dans le surréalisme*, Norway: Solum & Paris: Privat, 1982 (see index).

Bb1051   Fauré, Michel, Refs in *Histoire du surréalisme sous l'occupation*, Paris: La Table Ronde, 1982 (see index).

Bb1052   Favre, Yves-Alain, 'Structure et poésie de *L'Amour fou*', *Queste*, 1 (1984), 177–89.

Bb1053   Fernandez Zoïla, Adolfo, 'Mots en jeu / enjeu de mots', in *L'Évolution psychiatrique*, XLIV, 1 (jan.–mars 79), 29–42.

Bb1054   Fejtö, François, 'Il y a vingt ans, mourait AB', *France-Forum*, 233–34 (jan.–mars 87), 62–63.

Bb1055   Filliolet, Jacques, 'Sur les routes du style', in Ba87, pp.117–24.

Bb1056   Fingesten, Peter, 'Surrealism and the Symbolic Paradox', *Humanitas*, VIII, 2 (May 72), 209–19.*

Bb1057   Finkelstein, Haim N., '"L'objet insolite" in Breton's Writings', in J.-F. Dupuis ed., *Controstoria del surrealismo*, Rome: Arcana 1978, pp.15–28.*

Bb1058   Fontanella, Luigi, '*Les Champs magnétiques*, prima opera surrealista', *Terzio occhio*, IV, 12 (sept.78), 1–9.

Bb1059   Ford, Charles-Henri, 'Après-midi avec AB' [poem tr. by Serge Fauchereau], *Digraphe*, 30 (juin 83), 106–07.

Bb1060   Foster, Hal, 'L'Amour faux', *Art in America*, 6 (Jan.86), 116–28.*

Bb1061   Fouchet, Max-Pol, Ref. in *Fontaines de mes jours. Conversations avec Albert Mermoud*, Paris: Stock (Coll. 'Les Grands Auteurs'), 1979, pp.202–03.

Bb1062   Fourny, Jean-François, '"Un jour ou l'autre on saura": de dada au surréalisme', *Revue d'histoire littéraire de la France*, LXXXVI, 5 (sept.–oct.86), 865–75.

Bb1063   ——, 'A propos de la querelle Breton-Bataille', *ibid.*, LXXXIV, 3 (mai–juin 84), 432–38.

Bb1064   Fowlie, Wallace, Ref. in *Journal of Rehearsals. A Memoir*, Durham, N.C.: Duke U.P., 1977, p.97.*

Bb1065   Frémon, Jean, 'Dopo Breton', in Ba38, pp.163–64.

Bb1066   Gabelloni, Lino, 'L'oggetto surrealista: "la trouvaille" et l'aggeggio', *Il Verri*, 12 (dic.75), 36–58.*

Bb1067   ——, 'Il demone dell'analogia', as preface in *Nadja*, Turin, 1972.*

Bb1068   ——, 'La Ville comme texte', *Lingua e Stile*, XI, 2 (giugno 76), 269–92.

Bb1069   Garelli, Jacques, 'Première étude: AB', 'Structure temporelle du poème de Breton: "Le Verbe être"', and 'Étude de la dimension du monde du "Verbe être" de Breton', in *Le Recel et la dispersion. Essai sur le champ de lecture poétique*, Paris: Gallimard, 1978, pp.13–35, 131–42, and 143–51.

Bb1070   Gascoyne, David, Ref. in *Journal de Paris et d'ailleurs, 1936–1942*, Paris: Flammarion, 1984, pp.171–72.*

Bb1071   Gateau, Jean-Charles, 'Zinzolin', in *Abécédaire critique*, Geneva: Droz, 1987, pp.257–60.

Bb1072   Gateau, Jean-Charles & Georges Nivat, 'Les Surréalistes et l'U.R.S.S.: histoire d'une déclaration', *Les Cahiers du XXe siècle*, 4 (1975), 149–54. Introduction to Ab762.

Bb1073   Gaubert, Alain, 'Crise de "ver"', *Licorne* (Poitiers), 8 (1984), 31–47.

Bb1074   ——, '"L'énigme n'existe pas": ou ce que disait le groupe', *ibid.*, 9 (1985), 105–52.

Bb1075   Gaudin, Colette, 'Tours et détours négatifs dans "La confession dédaigneuse" de Breton', *Romanic Review*, LXXI, 4 (Nov.80), 394–412.

Bb1076   Gavronsky, Serge, 'Discours manifeste: AB', in *Culture écriture. Essais critiques*, Rome: Bulzoni, 1983, pp.59–78.

Bb1077   ——, 'Écrire l'amour: le surréalisme tel qu'en lui-même', in *Écrire l'homme. Surréalisme — humanisme — poétique*, Rome: Bulzoni, 1986, pp.37–61.

Bb1078   ——, 'Poétique du freinage: l'ambigu surréalisme', *Le Siècle éclaté*, 3 (1985), 21–38; also in *RLM: Histoire des idées et des littératures*, 720–25 (1985), 21–38.*

Bb1079   ——, 'Surrealism's unnamed manifesto', in *Manifestoes and Movements*, Columbia, S. Carolina: University of S. Carolina Press (French literature series, VII), 1980, pp.88–97.*

Bb1080   Geles, Dorina, 'AB', *Steaua* (Bucharest), XXIII, 21 (1–15 nov.72), unpag. [24, 27].

Bb1081   Gibs, Sylwia, 'Les fonctions de la parenthèse dans *Nadja* d'AB', in *Recherches en sciences des textes. Hommage à Pierre Albouy* (Université de Paris VII), Grenoble: Presses Universitaires de Grenoble, 1977, pp.181–88.

Bb1082   Gimenez Frontin, J.-L., Refs in *El Surrealismo. El tornon al movimento bretoniano*, Barcelona: Montesinos, 1983.*

Bb1083   Givone, Sergio, Refs in *Hybris e melancolia. Studi sulle poetiche del novecento*, Milan: U. Mursia (Coll. 'Saggi di estetica e di poetica'), 1974 (see index).

Bb1084   Goemans, Camille, Letters to AB (1927–29), in *Lettres surréalistes, Le Fait accompli*, 81–95 (mai–août 73), Brussels: Les Lèvres Nues, 1973.

Bb1085   Goldyka, Jadwiga, 'AB, romancier ou prosateur', *Romanica Wratislaviensia*, XIV, 416 (1979), 61–80.

Bb1086   Gollut, Jean-Daniel, '*Arcane 17*', in *Le Surréalisme dans le texte* [see Bb856], pp.297–307.

Bb1087   Gontier, Fernande, 'Vision mythique de la femme', in *La Femme et le couple dans le roman de l'entre-deux guerres*, Paris: Klincksieck, 1976, pp.101–25.

Bb1088   Gonzalez, 'AB: la via surrealista. — Semanal', *El Mundo* (Medellin), (27 sept.86), 4–5.*

Bb1089   Goujon, J.-P., 'Une dédicace inattendue', *Bulletin des amis de Pierre Louys*, 7 (sept.78), 2–4.

Bb1090   Goulet, Jacques, 'AB pour Maximilien Robespierre', *Les Cahiers rationalistes*, 320 (jan.76), 109–12.

Bb1091   Gourdon, Gilles, 'Portrait de l'artiste en apprenti-sorcier', in Ba67, pp.27–28.

Bb1092   Gratton, Johnnie, 'Poetics of the Surrealist Image', *Romanic Review*, LXIX, 1–2 (Jan.–March 78), 103–14.

Bb1093 Gratton, Johnnie, 'Runaway: Textual Dynamism in the Surrealist Poetry of AB', *Surrealism and Language, Forum for Modern Language Studies*, XVIII, 2 (Apr.82), 126–41; also in Ian Higgins, ed., *Surrealism and Language*, Edinburgh: Scottish Academic Press, 1986.

Bb1094 Grimm, Jürgen, 'AB — Philippe Soupault', *Das avantgardistische Theater Frankreichs, 1895–1930*, Munich: C.H.Beck, 1982, pp.254–68.*

Bb1095 Gross, Stefan, 'Maurice Maeterlinck und die Avantgarde: Maeterlinck — Artaud — Breton', in *Aspekte der Literatur des Fin-de-siècle in der Romania*, Angelika Corbineau-Hoffmann & Albert Gier, eds., Tübingen: Max Niemeyer, 1983, pp.201–25.

Bb1096 Grossmann, Simone, Refs in 'Le Poète et les pierres', *Marginales*, XXXVI, 199 (mai 81), 8–11.

Bb1097 ———, 'La rencontre de Gracq et de Breton', in *Julien Gracq et le surréalisme*, Paris: Corti, 1980, pp.13–17.

Bb1098 Guedj, Colette, '*Nadja* d'AB, ou l'exaltation réciproque du texte et de la photographie', *Les Mots la vie*, n.s. (1984), 91–136.

Bb1099 Guérin, Dominique, Refs in *La Politique de l'imaginaire*, Paris, The Hague: Mouton, 1974, *passim*.

Bb1100 Guigon, Emmanuel, & Edouard Jaguer, 'Autour du château étoilé', *Docsur, Documents sur le surréalisme* (Actual), 7 (mars 89), 8pp.*

Bb1101 Guilmette, Bernadette, '*Les Champs magnétiques* par AB et Philippe Soupault: images telluriques et cosmiques, leur classification et leur signification symbolique', *Co-incidences* (Ottawa), IV, 2 (mars–avr.74), 32–57.

Bb1102   Guillaume, Paul, ed., *Sculptures nègres. Collection AB et Paul Éluard*, New York: Hacker Art Books, 1973.

Bb1103   Guillon, Jean-Pierre, 'AB et la Bretagne', *Les Cahiers de l'Iroise*, XXXIV, 1 (jan.–mars 87), 1–7.

Bb1104   Gutt, Tom, 'L'Avant-dernier Abencérage', in Ba74, pp.19–21.

Bb1105   Hamblet, Edwin J., 'AB and the Montreal Automatistes', *Quebec Studies*, I, 1 (Spring 83), 257–67.*

Bb1106   Halpern, Joseph, 'Breton's Overheated Room', *French Forum*, VII, 1 (Jan.82), 46–57.

Bb1107   ——, 'Describing the Surreal', *Yale French Studies*, 61 (1981), 89–106.

Bb1108   Hedges, Duke Inez, 'Surrealist Metaphor: Frame Theory and Componential Analysis', *Poetics Today* (Tel Aviv) IV, 2 (1983), 275–95; also under title 'Surrealist metaphor and thought', in *Languages of Revolt: Dada and Surrealist Literature and Film*, Durham, N.Carolina: Duke U.P., 1983, pp.79–107.

Bb1109   Heijenoort, Jean van, 'Breton va voir Trotsky', *La Quinzaine littéraire*, 277 (16–30 avr.78), 10–11; also in *Sept ans auprès de Léon Trotsky*, Paris: Lettres Nouvelles, 1978, pp.178–90.

Bb1110   Heistein, Jozef, 'La Pensée littéraire de l'avant-garde. Du futurisme au premier manifeste de Breton', *Beiträge zur Romanischen Philologie*, XVI, 1 (1977), 79–82.

Bb1111   Helm, Michael, 'Surrealismen, marxismen og den indre erfaring' [Surrealism, Marxism and the Inner experience], *Vindrosen*, XX, 3 (1973), 2–12.*

Bb1112   Henein, Georges, 'L'Anti-Nadja', in Ba66, pp.14–15.

Bb1113   Henein, Georges, 'Avec AB', *Grid*, 5 (hiver 86–87), 42.*

Bb1114   ——, *L'Esprit frappeur (carnets 1940–1973)*, Paris: Encre 1980, pp.37, 69, 198.

Bb1115   Henri, Maurice, Letter to AB (24.3.51), in José Pierre, *Tracts surréalistes et déclarations collectives, II* [see Bb833], pp.86–101.

Bb1116   Hermann, Claudine, Ref. in *Les Voleuses de langue*, Paris: Des Femmes, 1976, pp.58–64.

Bb1117   Hillenaar, Henk, 'Nadja et Edwarda', in *Vitalité et contradictions* ... [see Bb920], pp.125–35.

Bb1118   Hilsum, Mireille, Refs in 'René Hilsum, un éditeur des années vingt', *Bulletin du bibliophile*, IV (1983), 460–74.

Bb1119   Hölz, Karl, 'Breton — die ontologische Begründung der Sprache', in *Destruktion und Konstruktion. Studien zum Sinnverstehen in der modernen französischen Literatur*, Frankfurt: Vittorio Klostermann (Coll. Analecta Romanica Heft 45), 1980, pp.69–116.

Bb1120   Houdebine, Jean-Louis, 'D'une Lettre en souffrance (Freud/Breton, 1938) première partie', *Promesse*, 32 (print.72), 85–96.

Bb1121   Hubert, Étienne-Alain, CR of Ba45, *Revue d'histoire littéraire de la France*, LXXVIII, 3 (mai–juin 78), 502–05.

         ——, see Bb904.

Bb1122   Hubert, Renée Riese, 'The Artbook as Poetic Code: Breton's Yves Tanguy', *L'Esprit créateur*, XXII, 4 (Winter 82), 56–66.

Bb1123   Hubert, Renée Riese, '*Nadja* depuis la mort de Breton', *Œuvres et critiques*, II, 1 (print.77), 93–102.

Bb1124   Hugnet, Georges, Refs in *Pleins et déliés. Souvenirs et témoignages 1926–1972*, Paris: Authier, 1972 (see index). Also contains Bb427, pp.323–45.

Bb1125   Ilie, Paul, 'The term "Surrealism" and its Philological Imperatives', *Romanic Review*, LXIX, 1–2 (Jan.–March 78), 90–102.

Bb1126   Ilutiu, Vicentiu, 'Le Surréalisme et la nostalgie de la totalité primordiale', in *Mircea Eliade et les horizons de la culture* (Actes du Colloque International d'Aix-en-Provence, 3–5 mai 84), Aix-en-Provence: Publications Universitaires de Provence, 1985, pp.283–93.

Bb1127   Isou, Isidore, reprint of Bb434, Paris: Centre de Créativité-Edition Littéraire, 1977.*

Bb1128   Jaguer, Edouard, 'AB, Cambiare la vita/cambiare la vista', tr. by Mirka Sapunzachi, *Terzo occhio* (Bologna), X, 30 (marzo 84), 11–14; also in French under title 'AB. Changer la vie — changer la vue', in Ba74, pp.32–43.

    ——, see Bb1100.

Bb1129   Janover, Louis, 'Breton/Blum: brève rencontre qui en dit long (du temps que les surréalistes étaient marxistes)', *Mélusine*, 8 (1986), 91–109.

Bb1130   ——, 'Breton et le surréalisme', and 'Breton et le nouveau matérialisme', in *Surréalisme, art et politique*, Paris: Galilée, 1980, pp.26–29 and 75–78.

Bb1131   Jean, Denis-J., 'AB and the "Déclaration du groupe surréaliste en Angleterre"', *Les Bonnes feuilles*, VI, 2 (print.77), 23-29.*

Bb1132   ——, 'An Invitation Refused: AB and Surrealism in England in 1959', *Dada/Surrealism*, 5 (1975), 77-79. Includes unpublished letter from Brunius to AB (1959), translated.

Bb1133   Jean, Georges, 'Anthologie permanente de la poésie. Les Poèmes d'AB', *Le Français aujourd'hui*, 28 (jan.75), 105-09.

Bb1134   Jean, Marcel, 'Les Pieds du garde-chasse' [poem], in Ba74, p.55.

Bb1135   Jenny, Laurent, 'La Surréalité et ses signes narratifs', *Poétique*, 16 (1973), 499-520.

Bb1136   ——, Refs in 'Les Aventures de l'automatisme', *Littérature*, 72 (déc.88), 3-11.

Bb1137   Jones, Louisa, '*Nadja* and the Language of Poetic Fiction', *Dada/Surrealism*, 3 (1973), 45-52.

Bb1138   Jouffroy, Alain, 'Le Modèle intérieur', *Le Surréalisme, XXe Siècle*, 42-43 (1975), unpag.

Bb1139   ——, Refs in *Le Roman vécu*, Paris: Laffont, 1978, pp.113-16, 148-67, 232-33, 248-49, 276-77, 311-17, 337-39, 353-67.

Bb1140   ——, Refs in *La Vie réinventée. L'explosion des années 20 à Paris*, Paris: Laffont, 1982, *passim*.

Bb1141   Joyeux, Marcel, Refs in *L'Anarchie dans la société contemporaine. Une hérésie nécessaire?*, Paris: Casterman, 1977, pp.62, 67, 75-76, 102.

Bb1142   Julliard, Suzanne, 'Le miroir la nuit', in *Rêve et rêverie*, Paris: Hachette (Coll. 'Thèmes et parcours littéraires'), 1973, pp.94–98.

Bb1143   Kalandra, Zavis, 'L'Acte d'AB', *Change*, 25 (1975), 58–60.

Bb1144   Kanters, Robert, 'Esotérisme et surréalisme', *Mélusine*, 2 (1981), 11–21.

Bb1145   Kapidžić-Osmanagić, Hanifa, 'AB ili žudnja za totalnošću' [AB or the Thirst for Totality], *Izraz* (Sarajevo), XXII, 10 (oct.78), 1269–1308.

Bb1146   ——, Refs in *Affrontements III: Ristic, Begic, Davico, Krleza*, Sarajevo: Svjetlost, 1986.*

Bb1147   Kaufman, Vincent, 'What are Breton's Women For?', tr. by Sally Silk, *SubStance 54*, XVI, 3 (1987), 57–68.*

Bb1148   Kerouredan, Henri G., 'Guillevic, Breton', in G.-E. Clancier, ed., *Clancier. Guillevic. Tortel*, Marseille: Sud, 1983, pp.154–58.

Bb1149   Kesting, Marianne, 'Der Protest gegen die reale Welt. Bretons Manifeste des Surrealismus', in *Auf der Suche nach der Realität. Kritische Schriften zur modernen Literatur*, Munich: R.Piper & Co.(Piper Paperback), 1972, pp.248–50.

Bb1150   Kirsch, Vicki, 'Ghost-Ridden Authors/ Ghost-Written Texts: Female Phantoms in Two Works by AB and Georges Bataille', *Paroles gelées* (UCLA), 5 (1987), 37–53.*

Bb1151   Knowlton, Edgar C., 'AB's "Rano Raraku"', *Explicator*, XL, 4 (Summer 82), 50–52.

Bb1152   Kochmann, René, '"Une maison peu solide": lecture d'un texte de Breton', *Australian Journal of French Studies*, XXI, 1 (Jan.–Apr. 84), 85–109.

Bb1153   Krauss, Rosalind E., Refs in 'The Photographic Conditions of Surrealism', *October*, 19 (Winter 1981), 3–34; also in *The Origins of the Avant-garde and Other Modernist Myths*, Cambridge, Mass. & London: MIT Press, pp.87–118; also tr. under title 'La Photographie et le surréalisme', *Critique*, XXXVIII, 426 (nov.82), 895–914.

Bb1154   Kritzman, Lawrence D., 'For a Structural Analysis of *Nadja*: A Scientific Experiment', *Rackman Literary Studies*, 4 (Spring 73), 9–23.

Bb1155   Kroymann, Maren, '"Déchiffrer la femme". Eine Lektüre von Bretons *Nadja*', *Lendemains*, VII, 25–26 (Feb.82), 168–76.

Bb1156   Kunstmann, Heinrich, 'Zur Polemik tschechischer Surrealisten mit I.Erenburg und zum Fall A.Breton: eine Dokumentation', *Die Welt der Slaven* (Munich), XXII (1977), 316–36.

Bb1157   Kyria, Pierre, 'AB derrière son mythe' [CR of Ba45], *Le Magazine littéraire*, 101 (juin 75), 54–56.

Bb1158   Labuda, Aleksander, 'L'Univers des personnes dans Le *Paysan de Paris* et dans *Nadja*', *Romanica Wratislaviensia*, VI, 140 (1971), 67–81.

Bb1159   La Charité, Virginia A., CR of Ba8, *French Review*, XLV, 4 (March 72), 912–93.

Bb1160   Ladimer, Bethany, 'Madness and the Irrational in the Work of AB: A Feminist Perspective', *Feminist Studies*, VI, 1 (Spring 80), 175–95.

Bb1161 Laffitte, Maryse, 'De l'atopie à l'utopie. Petit dialogue entre Baudelaire et Breton', *Revue romane*, XVIII, 1 (1983), 61–72.

Bb1162 ——, 'L'Image de la femme chez Breton: contradictions et virtualités', *ibid.*, XI, 2 (1976), 286–305.

Bb1163 Lamba, Jacqueline, 'Entretien avec Arturo Schwarz sur la rencontre Trotsky-Breton', *Les Lettres nouvelles*, 4 (sept.–oct.75), 99–111. Revised version of interview in Ba88.

Bb1164 Lamy, Suzanne, 'Breton-Duras. B.D. — Ma bande dessinée ou lecture d'une confluence', *Mélusine*, 4 (1983), 111–22.

Bb1165 ——, 'Le Lexique "traditionnel" d'*Arcane 17*', *Mélusine*, 2 (1981), 152–74.

Bb1166 Lane, Philippe, '"Une maison peu solide". Une lecture peu assurée', *Pratiques*, 39 (oct.83), 36–40.

Bb1167 Langowski, Gerald J., 'Los pasos perdidos: concepto surrealista de "le merveilleux"', in Donald A. Yates, ed., *Otros mundos otros fuegos: fantasía y realismo mágico en Iberoamerica*, East Lansing: Michigan State Univ., 1975, pp.211–15.*

Bb1168 Lanoux, Armand, 'Du Guy pour Breton', in Ba75, pp.8–10.

Bb1169 Lapacherie, Jean-Gérard, 'Breton critique d'Apollinaire: le calligramme comme bégaiement', *Que vlo-ve?*, 2e série, 14 (avr.–juin 85), 16–20.

Bb1170 ——, 'Un "topos" de la pensée du XVIIIe siècle dans les textes "théoriques" d'AB', *Mélusine*, 7 (1985), 219–24.

Bb1171 Lascault, Gilbert, 'L'Illustration surréaliste de l'égarement quotidien', *Le Surréalisme, XXe Siècle*, 42–43 (1975), unpag.

Bb1172   Laude, André, 'AB le magnifique', *Les Nouvelles littéraires*, LV, 2618 (12–19 jan.78), 32.

Bb1173   ——, 'Breton bariolé', *ibid.*, LIV, 2551 (23 sept.76), 4.

Launay, Michel, see Bb929.

Bb1174   Laurent, Marcel, 'Explication française. AB: le mythe de Mélusine (*Arcane 17*)', *L'École des lettres*, LXIII, 5 (13 nov.71), 23–26.

Bb1175   Lebel, Robert, 'De Dada au surréalisme', *Le Surréalisme, XXe Siècle*, 42–43 (1975), unpag.

Bb1176   ——, 'Marcel Duchamp et AB', in Ann d'Harnoncourt & K. McShine, eds., *Marcel Duchamp*, New York: MOMA, 1973.*

Bb1177   ——, Bb486, also as preface to Ba78, under title 'AB initiateur de la peinture surréaliste', pp.7–13.

Bb1178   Le Gars, Yves, 'Corps de la ville, corps du cosmos dans l'itinéraire moniste d'AB', *Les Cahiers du XXe siècle*, 4 (1975), 97–108.

Bb1179   ——, 'Le Poète et le révolutionnaire' [CR of Ba88], *La Quinzaine littéraire*, 269 (16 déc.77), 10–11.

Bb1180   Legrand, Gérard, 'AB, les idées et les idéologies', in Ba66, pp.18–21.

Bb1181   ——, 'L'Amour de la peinture', in Ba67, pp.52–55.

Bb1182   ——, 'Coups de foudre surréalistes', *Le Magazine littéraire*, 192 (fév.83), 22–23.

Bb1183   ——, 'Un non-anti-philosophe', in Ba87, pp.182–91.

Bb1184   Legrand, Gérard, José Pierre & Jean Schuster, 'Holà!' (15 fév.67), in José Pierre, *Tracts surréalistes et déclarations collectives, II* [see Bb833], pp.255-57.

Bb1185   Lehouck, E., 'La Lecture surréaliste de Charles Fourier', *Australian Journal of French Studies*, XX, 1 (Jan.-Apr.83), 26-36.

Bb1186   Leiris, Michel, 'Breton, le patron' [interview], *Le Nouvel observateur*, 1228 (20-26 mai 88), 62-63.

Bb1187   Lemaître, Maurice, Lettre to AB (14 mars 62), in *Sur Tristan Tzara, AB, Philippe Soupault*, Paris: Centre de Créativité, ed. Lettristes, 1980, unpag.

Bb1188   Leonard, Martine, 'Photographie et littérature: Zola, Breton, Simon (Hommage à Roland Barthes)', *Études françaises* (Montreal), XVIII, 3 (hiver 83), 93-108.

Bb1189   Leroy, Claude, 'Limites non-frontières entre humour et fantastique dans l'écriture surréaliste', *Europe*, 611 (mars 80), 65-72.

Bb1190   ——, 'L'Amour fou, même', in Ba75, pp.28-33; also in Ba83, pp.119-24.

Bb1191   Lévêque, Jean-Jacques, 'Les Deux Voies parallèles de la peinture surréaliste', *La Galerie*, 117 (juin 72), 44-46.

Bb1192   Leuwers, Daniel, 'Jouve, Breton et la psychanalyse', *NRF*, 323 (déc.79), 100-06.

Bb1193   Lévi-Strauss, Claude, Ref. in *Tristes tropiques* (Paris: Plon, 1955), Paris: Plon (Coll. 'Terre humaine'), 1984, p.20.

Bb1194   Levionnois, Louis, 'Breton et Mallarmé', *Le Surréalisme contestataire et contesté, Points et contrepoints*, 113 (déc.74), 53–60.

Bb1195   Levy, Karen D., 'AB and the artist's gesture', in Charles Nelson, ed., *Studies in Language and Literature*, Richmond: Eastern Kentucky Univ, pp.337–341.*

Bb1196   Levy, Sydney, 'AB's Nadja and Automatic Writing', *Dada/Surrealism*, 2 (1972), 28–31.

Bb1197   Liberati, André, 'Théorie et pratique de la poésie', in Ba87, pp.49–55.

Bb1198   Lienhard, Pierre-André, 'De Nadja à Mélusine: le génie féminin de la médiation', in *La Femme et le surréalisme* [see Bb949], pp.64–73.

Bb1199   Lima, Maria Isabel Pires de, 'Nadja — entre Melusina e Medusa', *Coloqio/Letras* (Portugal), 72 (mar.83), 41–50.

Bb1200   Limbour, Georges, 'Après la mort d'AB', in *Limbour l'irréductible*, Paris: Minuit, 1976, pp.781–82.*

Bb1201   ——, Extract from Bb669 under title 'La Charge contre AB' [Limbour given as sole author], *Le Monde [des livres]*, 9844 (17 sept.76), 18.

Bb1202   Linstrum, Cathy, '"L'Asile des femmes": Subjectivity and Femininity in Breton's *Nadja* and Wittig's *Le Corps lesbien*', *Nottingham French Studies*, XXVII, 1 (May 88), 35–45.

Bb1203   Loeb, Edouard, Refs in *Mon siècle sur un fil*, Paris: Laffont, 1982, pp.178, 220.

Bb1204   Lombardo, Patrizia, *Edgar Poe et la modernité*. *Breton, Barthes, Derrida, Blanchot*, Birmingham, Alabama: Summa Publ., 1985, pp.75–86.

Bb1205   Losfeld, Éric, Refs in *Endetté comme une mule ou la passion d'éditer*, Paris: Belfond, 1979, pp.14, 43–45, 48, 50–55, 81, 125.

Bb1206   Magritte, René, Bb515, also in *Écrits complets*, Paris: Flammarion, 1979, p.655.

Bb1207   ——, Letter to AB (11.8.46), *ibid.*, pp.200–01; also in *Le Fait accompli*, 51–53 (juin–août 71)*; also in *Manifestes et autres écrits*, Brussels: Les Lèvres Nues, pp.66–69.*

Bb1208   ——, Letter to AB (24.6.46), in *Lettres à Paul Nouget, Le Fait accompli*, 127–129 (nov.74), Bruxelles: Les Lèvres Nues; also in René Magritte, *Écrits complets* [see Bb1206], p.200.

Bb1209   Maille, Anick, 'Un Paradoxe lexicologique et idéologique: "Révolution Surréaliste"', *Mélusine*, 1 (1979), 74–91.

Bb1210   Malouvier, Guy, 'La "Faction" surréaliste des Canaries', *Le Puits de l'ermite*, 29–30–31 (mars 78), 36–37.

Bb1211   Manetti, Giovanni, 'Ready-made: semantica e pragmatica dell'umorismo dadaista e surrealista', *VS: Quaderni di Studi Semiotici*, 25 (genn.–apr.80), 65–86.*

Bb1212   Manka, Aleksandra, '*Les Champs magnétiques* ou l'écriture automatique mise en pratique', *Prace Historycznoliterackie* (Katowice), 22 (1983), 18–23.*

Bb1213   Manu, Emil, 'AB — Tristan Tzara în culisele congresului avangardei de la Paris' [Tristan Tzara in the Wings of the Paris Congress on the Avantgarde], *Manuscriptum* (Bucarest), IX, 1 (1978), 133–40.

Bb1214   ——, 'Insurectia de la Paris din 1922 (Polemica Breton-Tzara)' [The Paris 1922 Insurrection (The Breton-Tzara Polemic)], *Revista de istorie si theorie literara* (Bucarest), XXVI, 2 (1977), 271–88.

Bb1215   Marchand, Jean José, 'Un événement: le facsimilé du manuscrit des *Champs magnétiques*', *La Quinzaine littéraire*, 522 (16–31 déc.88), 18–19.

Bb1216   Margonari, Renzo, 'Una forma nuova di sensibilità', in Ba38, pp.51–74.

Bb1217   Mariën, Marcel, 'Mort de Nadja', *Le Fait accompli*, 12 (fév.75), unpag.*

Bb1218   Marissel, André, CR of Ba1, *Esprit*, XL, 412 (mars 72), 517–19.

Bb1219   Martin, Claude, '*Nadja* et le mieux-dire', *Revue d'histoire littéraire de la France*, LXXII, 2 (mars–avr.72), 274–86.

Bb1220   Martin, Graham Dunstan, 'A Measure of Distance: The Rhetoric of the Surrealist Adjective', in *Surrealism and Language* [see Bb1095], pp.108–25.

Bb1221   Mary, Georges, 'Les Deux Convulsions de Nadja ou le livre soufflé', *Mélusine*, 3 (1982), 207–14.

Bb1222   ——, 'Mélusine ou le lieu d'un change: La dynamique des figures dans *Arcane 17*', *Poétique*, 60 (nov.84), 489–98.

Bb1223 Matthews, J.H., 'AB already?' [CR of Ba4 and Ba8], *Modern Language Quarterly*, XXXIII, 3 (Sept.72), 327–34.

Bb1224 ——, 'AB and Joan Miró: *Constellations*', *Symposium*, XXXIV, 4 (Winter 80/81), 353–76.

Bb1225 ——, 'AB and Malcolm de Chazal: Perception versus Opacity', *Open Letter*, 2nd series, 5 (Summer 73), 164–73*; also in *Writing in a Modern Temper* [see Bb853], pp.164–173.

Bb1226 ——, 'AB and Painting: The Case of Arshile Gorky', in Ba53, pp.36–45.

Bb1227 ——, 'AB and Philippe Soupault', in *Theatre in Dada and Surrealism*, Syracuse, New York: Syracuse U.P., 1974, pp.85–108.

Bb1228 ——, 'AB, Jacques Brunius, and Surrealism in England', *Dada/Surrealism*, 6 (1976), 5–9.

Bb1229 ——, '"Balayer d'un mince projecteur un fragment du devenir": Surrealist Creativity and Criticism', *Symposium*, XXXVII, 1 (Spring 83), 48–67.

Bb1230 ——, Refs in *Benjamin Péret*, Boston: Twayne (Twayne's World Authors Series, 359), 1975 (see index).

Bb1231 ——, '"Une Contrée où le désir est roi": *L'Amour fou* d'AB', *Symposium*, XXXIII, 1 (79), 25–40.

Bb1232 ——, 'Désir et merveilleux dans *Nadja* d'AB', *Symposium*, XXVII, 3 (Fall 73), 246–68.

Bb1233 ——, '"Le désir qui ne se refuse rien" — *Les Vases communicants* d'AB', *Symposium*, XXXI, 3 (Fall 77), 212–30.

Bb1234   Matthews, J.H., 'Fifty Years later: The *Manifesto of Surrealism*', *Twentieth Century Literature*, XXI, 1 (Feb.75), 1–9.

Bb1235   ——, '*Manifeste du surréalisme*', and 'AB: *Anthologie de l'humour noir*', in *Towards the Poetics of Surrealism*, New York: Syracuse U.P., 1976, pp.68–83 and 88–101.

Bb1236   ——, CR of Ba91, in *French Forum*, VII, 1 (Jan.82), 85–86.

Bb1237   Matic, Dusan, extracts from Ba71, in *Fata Morgana 1966–76*, Paris: Fata Morgana, UGE (Coll. '10/18'), 1976, pp.175–81.

Bb1238   Matvejevitch, Predrag, Refs in *Pour une poétique de l'événement. La poésie de circonstance*, Paris: UGE (Coll. '10/18'), 1979, pp.161–63, 269.

Bb1239   Mauriac, Claude, 'Du nouveau sur AB', *Le Figaro littéraire*, 1486 (9 nov.74), 13.

Bb1240   ——, 'AB et la subversion du langage'[CR of Ba46], *Le Figaro littéraire*, 1527 (23 aout 75), II, 10.

Bb1241   Mead, Gerald, Refs in *The Surrealist Image: A Stylistic Study*, Bern & Las Vegas: Peter Lang (Utah Studies in Literature and Linguistics, 9) 1978, *passim*.

Bb1242   ——, 'A Syntactic Model in Surrealist Style', *Dada/Surrealism*, 2 (1972), 33–37.

Bb1243   Ménil, René, 'Sur la Préface de Breton au *Cahier d'un retour au pays natal*', in *Tracées, identité, négritude, esthétique aux Antilles*, Paris: Laffont (Coll. 'Chemins d'identité'), 1981, pp.201–212.

Bb1244   Menis, Carla, 'Gli alchimisti mentali', in Ba38, pp.75–88.

Bb1245   Mercier, André, 'AB et l'ordre figuratif dans les années 20', in *Le Retour à l'ordre dans les arts plastiques et l'architecture, 1919–1925*, C.I.E.R.E.C. (St Étienne), Travaux VIII (1975), pp.277–316.

Bb1246   Merrim, Stephanie, 'Dario and Breton: Two Enigmas', *Latin American Literary Review* (Pittsburgh), IV, 9 (Fall–Winter 76), 48–62.

Bb1247   Metzidakis, Stamos, 'Breton and Poetic Originality', in Ba53, pp.28–35.

Bb1248   ———, 'Picking up Narrative Pieces in a Surrealist Prose Poem', *Orbis Litterarum*, XL, 4 (1985), 317–26.

Bb1249   Meunier, Jacques, 'Les Poupées Hopi', in Ba67, pp.41–42.

Bb1250   Michaud, Stéphane, Refs in '"Un brasier d'images": Novalis dans le surréalisme', in *Du Romantisme au surnaturalisme. Hommage à Claude Pichois*, Neuchâtel: La Baconnière, 1985, pp.297–314.

Bb1251   Mingelgrün, Albert, '"Tournesol" d'AB: étude d'un poème-récit', *L'Information littéraire*, XL, 2 (mars–sept.88), 30–35.

Bb1252   Modiano, Patrick & Emmanuel Berl, Refs in *Interrogatoire*, Paris: Gallimard (Coll. 'Témoins'), 1976, pp.40, 46–47, 117–18.

Bb1253   Morel, Jean-Paul, 'Breton and Freud', *Diacritics*, II, 2 (Summer 72), 18–26.

Bb1254   Morel, Jean-Pierre, 'Aurélia, Gradiva, X: Psychanalyse et poésie dans *Les Vases communicants*', *Revue de littérature comparée*, XLVI, 1 (jan.–mars 72), 68–89.

Bb1255   Motte, Warren F., Jr., 'Metaliterary Games in *Nadja*', *Symposium*, XLII, 3 (Fall 88), 232–45.

Bb1256   Mounin, Georges, Bb576, also in *Camarade poète*, I, Paris: Galilée/Oswald (Coll. 'Écritures/figures'), 1979, pp.9–14.

Bb1257   Mourier-Casile, Pascaline, 'Mélusine ou la triple en phase: Fée, Lilith, Phé dans *Arcane 17*', *Mélusine*, 2 (1981), 175–202.

Bb1258   ——, 'Du pagure à l'agate: "On longe toujours le bruit de la mer"', in Ba87, pp.141–53.

Bb1259   Mundwiler, Leslie, 'Williams, Breton, Marcuse, Foucault', *Open Letter*, II, 5 (Summer 73), 54–68.*

Bb1260   Murciano, Carlos, '*Los Pasos perdidos* de AB', *Poesia hispánica*, 239 (nov.72), 10–11.

Bb1261   Muzard, Suzanne, untitled text, in Marcel Jean, *Autobiographie du surréalisme*, Paris: Seuil, 1978, pp.31–34.

Bb1262   Nadeau, Maurice, 'Breton dans la Pléiade', *La Quinzaine littéraire*, 511 (16–30 juin 88), 5–6.

Bb1263   Navarri, Roger, '"Au grand jour"/"A la grande nuit", ou la double postulation de la critique surréaliste', *L'Information littéraire*, XXXIII, 2 (mars–avr.81), 65–68.

Bb1264   ——, '*Nadja* ou l'écriture malheureuse', *Europe*, LI, 528 (avr.73), 186–95.

Bb1265   Nel, Noël, 'Le Château imaginaire d'AB', *La Barbacane*, 13/14 (1972), 23–36.

Bb1266   Neyer, Hans Joachim, 'Dichtung und Warenwelt bei Aragon und Breton (1916–1922)', *Lendemains*, III, 9 (jan.78), 16–34.

Bb1267 Nezval, Vitezslav, *Ulice Gît-le-Cœur*, Prague, 1936; tr. under title *Rue Gît-le-Cœur*, tr. Katia Krivanek, La Tour d'Aigues: Éditions de L'Aube, 1988, *passim*.

Nivat, Georges, see Bb1072.

Bb1268 Noël, Bernard, Refs in *Marseille–New York, 1940–1944, une liaison surréaliste*, [bilingual edn], Marseille: André Dimanche, 1985.*

Bb1269 ——, 'L'Œil surréaliste', in *La Planète affolée* [see Bb1007], pp.15–24.

Bb1270 Nougé, Paul, 'D'une lettre à AB', in Christian Bussy, *Anthologie du surréalisme en Belgique*, Paris: Gallimard, 1972*; also in *Histoire de ne pas rire*, Lausanne: L'Age d'Homme (Coll. 'Lettres différentes'), 1980, p.79.

——, Letters to AB (avr.27–déc.32), in Ab749.

Bb1271 Novaković, Jelena, 'Bretonova poetika imaginarnog: Simboličke funkcije vatre' [Breton's poetics of the imaginary: the symbolic functions of fire], *Izraz* (Sarajevo), XXXI, 7–8 (Juli–Avg.87), 120–40.

Bb1272 ——, 'Bretonovo "Ogledalo čudesnog"'[Breton's "Mirror of the Marvelous"], *ibid.*, XXIX, 12 (Dec.85), 623–37.

Bb1273 ——, 'Les Éléments du fantastique et du merveilleux dans la poétique de Breton', *Gradina* (Belgrade), 7–8 (1988), 19–28.*

Bb1274 ——, Figures mythiques dans les romans poétiques de Breton: Mélusine', *Anali Filososkog Fakulteta*, XVIII (1987), 63–81. [Summary in French.]*

Bb1275   Novaković, Jelena, 'Prostorni vidovi Bretonovog imaginarnog sveta' [Perspectives on Breton's imaginary world], *Izraz* (Sarajevo), XXXII, 9–10 (Sept.–Okt.88), 639–58.

Bb1276   ——, CR of Aa839, *Knizevnakritika* (Belgrade), 1 (1989), 151–52.*

Bb1277   Nussbaum, 'Breton's *Nadja* and Aragon's *Le Paysan de Paris*: Evaluation of Two Surrealist Non-Novels', *Proceedings of the Pacific Northwest Conference on Foreign Languages* (Pullman), XXVI, 1 (1975), 92–97.*

Bb1278   Orenstein, Gloria Feman, 'The dialectics of transformation: AB, Antonin Artaud', in *The Theater of the Marvelous. Surrealism and the Contemporary Stage*, New York: New York U.P., 1975, pp.17–30.

Bb1279   ——, '*Nadja* Revisited: A Feminist Approach', *Dada/Surrealism*, 8 (1978), 91–106.

Bb1280   ——, 'Reclaiming the Great Mother: A Feminist Journey to Madness and Back in Search of a Goddess Heritage', *Symposium*, XXXVI, 1 (Spring 82), 45–70.

Bb1281   Oster, Daniel, 'AB ou le chanteur de Mexico', in *Passages de Zénon. Essai sur l'espace et les croyances littéraires*, Paris: Seuil, 1983, pp.98–99.

Bb1282   ——, 'Breton avant le mythe' [CR of Ba43], *Les Nouvelles littéraires*, LIII, 2487 (26 mai–1 juin 75), 3.

Bb1283   Oxenhandler, Neal, 'Cocteau, Breton and Ponge: The Situation of the Self', in *About French Poetry...* [see Bb851], pp.54–68.

Bb1284   ——, CR of Ba25, *French Review*, XLVI, 2 (Dec.72), 421–42.

Bb1285   Pabst, Walter, 'AB: "Saisons". (Breton/Soupault: *Les Champs magnétiques*, 2)', in *Die Moderne französische Lyrik. Interpretationen*, Berlin: Erich Schmidt, 1976, pp.140–60.

Bb1286   ——, Refs in *Französische Lyrik des zwanzigsten Jahrhunderts. Theorie und Dichtung der Avantgarden, Grundlagen der Romanistik*, Berlin: Erich Schmidt, 1983, pp.181–82, 197–205, 224–32.

Bb1287   Palayret, Guy, 'Attirances et répulsions: Aragon, Breton et les écrivains révolutionnaires autour du PCF (1930–1935)', *Mélusine*, 5 (1983), 79–100.

Bb1288   Parenti, Claire, 'Relire les manifestes', *Le Magazine littéraire*, 91–92 (sept.74), 19.

Bb1289   Parmentier, Michel A., 'AB et la question de l'unité du psychisme', *Australian Journal of French Studies*, XX, 1 (Jan.–Apr.83), 50–60.

Bb1290   ——, 'La Visée thérapeutique du surréalisme', *Mosaic*, XV, 3 (Sept.82), 63–77.

Bb1291   Passeron, René, 'Une dialectique de la création', in Ba87, pp.106–12.

Bb1292   Pastoureau, Henri, 'Aide-mémoire relatif à l'affaire Carrouges' (28 fév.51), in José Pierre, *Tracts surréalistes et déclarations collectives, II* [see Bb833], pp.51–63.

Bb1293   ——, 'AB, l'homme que j'ai connu', *L'Orne littéraire*, 3 (jan.83), 3–20.

Bb1294   ——, 'Entretien avec G. Bertin sur le surréalisme. Juin 1986', in Ba74, pp.24–30.

Bb1295   Pastoureau, Henri, 'Fragments analytiques', in Ba87, pp.17–32.

Bb1296   ——, Bb599, under title 'Interprétation du poème d'AB: "Forêt Noire"', with very minor modifications made by AB, *L'Orne littéraire*, 4 (print.83), 43–50.

Bb1297   ——, 'Observations relatives à l'opuscule de Breton-Péret: "L'Affaire Pastoureau et cie"' et au compte rendu de l'assemblée du 19 mars 1951' (23 mars 51), in José Pierre, *Tracts surréalistes et déclarations collectives, II* [see Bb833], pp.76–86.

Bb1298   ——, Refs in 'Remarques d'H.P. sur le tome 2 des *Tracts surréalistes et déclarations collectives, Champs des Activités Surréalistes*, n.s. (fév.83), 5–19.

Patin, Marc, see Bb833.

Bb1299   Paz, Octavio, Bb616, also under title 'AB, o la búsqueda de comenzio', in *La Búsqueda de Comenzio (escritos sobre el surrealismo)*, Madrid: Fundamentos (Coll. 'Espiral'), 1974, 1980; also under title 'AB and the search for the beginning', tr. Michael Schmidt, *PN Review*, XI, 4 (1984), 26–29.

Bb1300   Paulhan, Claire, 'Breton prend le large', *Le Monde [aujourd'hui]*, 12811 (6–7 avr.86), X.

Bb1301   Pellat, Jean-Christophe, 'L'Emploi des temps dans un texte narratif: AB, *L'Amour fou*, chapitre IV', *L'Information grammaticale*, XXXIV (juin 87), 31–35.

Bb1302   Penning, Dieter, 'Der Begriff der Überwirklichkeit. Nerval, Maupassant, Breton', in Christian W. Thomsen & Jens Malte Fischer, eds., *Phantastik in Literatur und Kunst*, Darmstadt: Wissenschaftliche Buchgesellschaft, 1980, pp.201–18.

Bb1303   Periz, Didier, 'Autour de *Légitime défense*', *Docsur, Documents sur le surréalisme* (Actual), 4 (oct.87), 4pp.*

Bb1304   Perloff, Marjorie, Refs in *The Poetics of Indeterminacy: Rimbaud to Cage*, Princeton, New Jersey: Princeton U.P., 1981 (see index).

Bb1305   Perniola, Mario, 'La trasgressione del surrealismo', in *Studi sul surrealismo* [see Bb889], pp.336–50.

Bb1306   Péret, Benjamin, 'Portrait of AB' [poem], *Malahat Review*, 51 (July 75), 54.*

Bb1307   Perros, Georges, Bb623 also in *Lectures. Comptes rendus et articles critiques*, Cognac: Le Temps qu'il fait (Coll. 'Multigraphies', 9), 1981, pp.25–27.

Bb1308   Pestino, Joseph F., 'Mario de Andrade and AB: Strange Bedfellows', *Tinta* (Santa Barbara), I, 4 (Summer 84), 15–20.*

Bb1309   Pfeiffer, Jean, 'La Médiatrice', *Obliques*, 14–15 (1977), 13–17.*

Bb1310   Picabia, Francis, Bb629 also in *Écrits*, II, Paris: Belfond 1978, p.152.

Bb1311   Pierre, José, '"Ainsi est la beauté"', in Ba87, pp.125–34; also tr. under title '"Such is beauty". The "Convulsive" in Breton's Ethics and Aesthetics', in Ba53, pp.19–27.

Bb1312   ——, 'Alfred Jarry, AB et la peinture', in Henri Bordillon, ed., *Alfred Jarry* (Cerisy 1981), Paris: Belfond, 1985, pp.111–25.

Bb1313   ——, 'AB et la peinture', *L'Information littéraire*, XXXII, 2 (mars–avr.80), 68–71.

Bb1314   Pierre, José, 'AB et le "poème-objet"', in *L'Objet au défi* [see Bb981], pp.131–42.

Bb1315   ——, 'AB et/ou "Minotaure"', in *Regards sur Minotaure. La Revue à tête de bête*', Geneva: Musée d'Art et d'Histoire, 1987, pp.95–119; also tr. under title 'AB and/or "Minotaure"', in *Focus on Minotaure. The Animal-Headed Review*, Geneva: Musée d'Art et d'Histoire, 1987, pp.95–119 [Exhib.cat.].

Bb1316   ——, 'Breton et Dali', in *Salvador Dali. Rétrospective 1920–1980*, Paris: Centre Georges Pompidou, Centre National d'Art Moderne, 1979, pp.131–40 [Exhib.cat.].

Bb1317   ——, 'Gustave Moreau et AB', *Coupure*, 7 (juin 72).*

Bb1318   ——, 'Le Lyrisme exalté ou refusé: Breton et les dadaïstes zurichois', *Champs des activités surréalistes*, 16 (juin 82), 41–57.

Bb1319   ——, 'La Pratique de la poésie', in Ba67, pp.31–34.

Bb1320   ——, 'Le "problème de la femme" dans le surréalisme' ('AB et "la grande promesse"', pp.32–38), in *La Femme et le surréalisme* [see Bb949], pp.32–63.

          ——, see Bb1184.

Bb1321   Pieyre de Mandiargues, André, Refs in *Le Désordre de la mémoire: entretiens avec Francine Mallet*, Paris: Gallimard, 1975, pp.108–44.

Bb1322   ——, 'A propos de *Chagrin d'amour*. Des analogies avec AB', *Les Nouvelles littéraires*, LIII, 2464 (16–22 déc.74), 4.

Bb1323   ——, 'A proposito di AB', in Ba38, pp.165–67.

Bb1324   Pillet, Alain-Pierre, 'AB à Venise: le plaisir d'une enquête', in *Du surréalisme et du plaisir* [see Bb981], pp.251–60.

Bb1325   Piper, David, 'The Savage Eye' [CR of At947], *The Guardian* (26 Oct.72), 14.

Bb1326   Pleynet, Marcelin, Refs in 'De la culture moderne', in *Paris-New York*, Paris: Centre Pompidou & MNAM, 1977, pp.115–123 (AB and Freud, pp.119–21) [Exhib.cat.].

Bb1327   ——, 'La Peinture et *Le Surréalisme et la peinture*', in *Art et littérature*, Paris: Seuil (Coll. 'Tel Quel'), 1977, pp.366–86; also tr. under title 'Painting and *Surrealism and Painting*', tr. Paul Rodgers, *Comparative Criticism*, 4 (1982), 35–53.

Bb1328   ——, Refs in *Transculture. Entretiens, essais et conférences*, Paris: UGE (Coll. '10/18'), 1979, pp.237, 242, 267–76, 302–04.

Bb1329   Plisnier, Charles, Letter to AB (1929), *Marginales*, XXVII, 150 (déc.72), 78–88.

Bb1330   Plocher, Hanspeter, 'Der verlorene Vater: Roger Vitracs *Victor ou les enfants du pouvoir* (1928) als Parodie des ersten surrealistischen Manifests', *Romanistisches Jahrbuch*, 32 (1981), 117–32.

Bb1331   ——, 'Vision und Wirklichkeit. AB als Interpret seiner Dichtung', *Zeitschrift für französische Sprache und Literatur*, 4 (1977), 143–59.

Bb1332   Plottel, Jeanine Parisier, 'Surrealist Archives of Anxiety', *The Anxiety of Anticipation*, *Yale French Studies*, 66 (1984), 121–34.

Bb1333   Plouvier, Paule, 'De l'utilisation de la notion freudienne de *sublimation* par AB', *Pleine marge*, 5 (juin 87), 41–51.

Bb1334   Plouvier, Paule, 'Utopie de la réalité, réalité de l'utopie', *Mélusine*, VII (1985), 87–99.

Bb1335   ——, 'Valéry et les surréalistes face au problème du rêve', *Bulletin des études valéryennes*, VI, 22 (jan.80), 51–60.

Bb1336   Plumyène, Jean, 'Paris surréel', *Commentaire*, VI, 21 (print.83), 217–20, and 23 (aut.83), 645–51; also in *Trajets parisiens*, Paris: Julliard, 1984, pp.91–129.

Bb1337   Pompili, Bruno, 'La lettura dell'evento in *L'Amour fou* di AB', *Si e No*, I, 3 (nov.74), 240–54.

Bb1338   Ponge, Francis, 'AB/Francis Ponge (fragments d'un dialogue 1952)', *Poésie 84*, 3 (mai–juin 84), 50–52.*

Bb1339   ——, Ref. in *Pratiques d'écriture ou l'inachèvement perpetuel*, Paris: Hermann, 1984, p.124.

Bb1340   Pontalis, J.-B., 'Les Vases non communicants', *NRF*, 302 (mars 78), 26–45.

Bb1341   Pop, Ion, 'În Vîntul eventualului' [In the wind of the possible], *Steaua* (Bucharest), XXV, 7 (julie 74), unpag. [43].

Bb1342   Porter, Laurence M., ' "L'Amour fou" and Individuation: A Jungian Reading of Breton's *Nadja*', *L'Esprit créateur*, XXII, 2 (Summer 82), 25–34.

Bb1343   Pouget, Christine, Refs in 'L'Attrait de la parapsychologie ou la tentation expérimentale', *Mélusine*, 2 (1981), 70–97.

Bb1344   ——, 'La Séduction de l'irrationnel', in Ba87, pp.163–71.

Bb1345   Poulet, Robert, 'AB (1896–1966)', in *Billets de sortie*, Paris: Nouvelles Éditions Latines, 1975, 107–10.*

Bb1346   Powrie, Phil, 'Automatic Writing: Breton, Daumal, Hegel', *French Studies* , XLII, 2 (Apr.88), 177–93.

Bb1347   ——, CR of Ba48 and Ba73, *ibid.*, pp.232–33.

Bb1348   Prassinos, Gisèle, Refs in *La Colline enchantée*, Paris: Grasset, 1983.*

Bb1349   Prébost, Jacques, 'Saint-Cirq-la-Popie et le souvenir d'AB', *Plaisir de France*, X, 420 (juin 74), 14–19.

Bb1350   Prevel, Jacques, *En compagnie d'Antonin Artaud*, Paris: Flammarion, 1974, pp.16–23, *passim*. Quotes letters from Artaud to AB, pp.111, 128.

Bb1351   Prigioni, Pierre, 'La Ligne narrative active-passive de *Poisson soluble*', *Gradiva*, 3 (1972), 5–7.

Bb1352   Prince, Gerald, 'La Fonction métanarrative dans *Nadja*', *French Review*, XLIX, 3 (Feb.76), 342–46.

Bb1353   ——, CR of Ba59, *ibid.*, LII, 5 (Apr.79), 781.

Bb1354   Py, Françoise, 'Les pigments et les mots', in Ba87, pp.99–105.

Bb1355   Quérière, Yves de la, 'Les Chaînes verbales de "L'Union libre"', *Teaching Language Through Literature*, XXIV, 1 (Dec.84), 11–25.*

Bb1356   Qvarnstrom, Gunnar, 'Surrealismen Manifesterar sig.', *Lyrikvannen* (Stockholm), 4 (1973), 34–43.*

Bb1357   Raba, Gyorgy, 'Il poetà Breton entra nel museo', in Ba38, pp.168–69.

Bb1358   Rabourdin, Dominique, 'Attitudes politiques', in Ba67, pp.48–51.

Bb1359   Racine, Nicole, 'BRETON André Robert', in *Dictionnaire biographique du mouvement ouvrier français*, Jean Maitron, ed., Tome 20, Paris: Les Éditions ouvrières, 1983, pp.260–64.

Bb1360   Raible, Wolfgang, 'AB: "l'Union libre"', in *Moderne Lyrik in Frankreich. Darstellung und Interpretationen*, Stuttgart, Berlin, Cologne & Mainz: W.Kohlhammer, 1972, pp.106–09.

Bb1361   Raillard, Georges, 'Breton en regard de Miró: *Constellations*', *Littérature*, 17 (fév.75), 3–13.

Bb1362   ———, 'Comment Breton s'approprie les *Constellations* de Miró', *Opus International*, 58 (Feb.76), 52–60 (also contains extract from Aa605 under title 'Un cycle parfait'); also in *Poésie et peinture du symbolisme au surréalisme en France et en Pologne*, *Les Cahiers de Varsovie*, 5 (1978), 171–80.

Bb1363   ———, Refs in 'Marseille passage du surréalisme', in *La Planète affolée* [see Bb1007], pp.47–55.

Bb1364   ———, 'On signe ici', *Littérature*, 25 (fév.77), 3–18.

Bb1365   Reboul, Jacquette, 'AB ou la quête du Graal', *Critique universitaire et critique créatrice*, Paris: Aux Amateurs de Livres, 1986, pp.39–65.

Bb1366   Reyer, Georges, 'El amor loco de AB', *Vanidades continentales* (Mexico), (nov.76), 38–40.*

Bb1367   Ribemont-Dessaignes, Georges *et al*, Bb669, also in José Pierre, *Tracts surréalistes et déclarations collectives 1922–1969. Tome I: 1922–1939*, Paris: Losfeld/Le Terrain Vague, 1980, pp.133–48.

Bb1368   Richer, Jean, Bb672, under title 'AB dans la forêt des signes', also in *Aspects ésotériques de l'œuvre littéraire*, Paris: Dervy-Livres (Coll. 'l'œuvre secrète'), 1980, pp.287–94.

———, see Bb1046.

Bb1369   Richter, Mario, '*Nadja* di AB. Analisi della prima sequenza', *Rivista di letterature moderne e comparate*, XXXVI, n.s., 3 (luglio–sett.83), 261–77; also tr. under title '*Nadja* d'AB: analyse de la première séquence', *Zeitschrift für französische Sprache und Literatur*, XCVI, 3 (1986), 225–37.

Bb1370   Rieuneau, Maurice, CR of Ba43, *Studi francesi*, XX, 59, fasc.II (magg.–agosto 76), 320–22.

Bb1371   Riffaterre, Michael, 'Semantic Overdetermination in Poetry', *PTL: A Journal for Descriptive Poetics and Theory of Literature*, II, 1 (Jan.77), 1–19.*

Bb1372   ———, 'Semantic incompatibilities in automatic writing', in *About French Poetry*... [see Bb851], pp.223–41; also in *Le Manifeste et le caché, Le Siècle éclaté*, 3 (1974), 41–62.

Bb1373   ———, Refs in *The Semiotics of Poetry*, Bloomington & London: Indiana U.P., 1978 (see index).

Bb1374   ———, 'The Surrealist Libido: AB's "*Poisson soluble*, No.8"', in Ba53, pp.59–66.

Bb1375   Rioux, Gilles, 'A propos des expositions internationales du surréalisme. Un document de 1947 et quelques considérations', *Gazette des beaux-arts*, XCI, 1311 (avr. 78), 163–71.

Bb1376   Risset, Jacqueline, 'AB: un surrealismo socialista?', *Quaderni storici*, 34 (genn.–apr.77), 124–34.

Bb1377   Risset, Jacqueline, 'I Discepoli di Breton: paradossi di un'avanguardia inattuale', *Quaderni portoghesi* (Rome), 3 (prima.78), 81–88.

Bb1378   Robert, Bernard-Paul, 'A propos d'AB', *Revue de l'Université d'Ottawa*, XLVI, 1 (jan.–mars 76), 128–44.

Bb1379   ——, 'AB et la parole intérieure', *ibid.*, XLIV, 3 (juil.–sept.74), 281–301.

Bb1380   ——, Breton, Engels et le matérialisme dialectique', *ibid.*, XLVI, 3 (juil.–sept.76), 293–308.

Bb1381   ——, 'Breton, Engels et le surréel', *ibid.*, XLIV, 1 (jan.–mars 74), 44–48.

Bb1382   ——, 'Origines du surréalisme', *ibid.*, LII, 2 (avr.–juin 82), 190–205.

Bb1383   ——, 'Pour une définition du surréalisme', *ibid.*, XLIII, 2 (avr.–juin 73), 297–306.

Bb1384   ——, 'Profils de "la fuite des idées" et surréalisme', *ibid.*, XLVII, 3 (juil.–sept.77), 345–64.

Bb1385   ——, 'Querelles et excommunications', *ibid.*, XLIV, 4 (oct.–déc.74), 475–86.

Bb1386   ——, 'Le Surréalisme désocculté', *ibid.*, XLIII, 3 (juil.–sept.73), 462–79.

Bb1387   ——, 'Surréalisme, métapsychique et psychiatrie classique', *Studi francesi*, XXI, 63, fasc.III (1977), 498–500.

Bb1388   Roche, Gérard, Introduction to Ba57*; shortened and altered version under title 'Breton, Trotsky: une collaboration', *Pleine marge*, 3 (mai 86), 73–93. Includes extracts of unpublished letters from Breton to Trotsky and Dwight McDonald.

———, see Ad814.

Bb1389   ———, 'Autour du quarantième anniversaire de la Révolution d'octobre: un débat révolutionnaire entre trotskystes et surréalistes', *Champs des activités surréalistes*, 18 (juin 83), 53–64.

Bb1390   ———, '"Changer la vie", "Transformer le monde"', in Ba87, pp.172–81.

Bb1391   ———, 'La Rencontre de l'aigle et du lion. Trotsky, Breton et le manifeste de Mexico', *Trotsky et les écrivains français*, *Cahiers Léon Trotsky*, 25 (mars 86), 22–46.

Bb1392   Rodriguez, Jean-François, 'Aragon, Breton et le débat autour de la "circonstance" en poésie', in *Letterature e ricerche*, Padova: Università di Padova (Quaderna della Scuola di Perfezionamento in Lingue e Letture Straniere, 3), 1982, pp.97–185.*

Bb1393   Ronat, Mitsou, 'Quand la langue manifeste', in *La Langue manifeste. Littérature et théorie du langage*, Paris: Action poétique, 1975, suppl. of *Action Poétique*, 63 (1975), 81–88.*

Bb1394   Rose, Alan, 'For an Independent Revolutionary Art: AB's Manifesto with Leon Trotsky', *European Studies Journal* (Cedar Falls), II, 1 (1985), 52–61.*

Bb1395   Rosenthal, Gérard, Refs in *Avocat de Trotsky*, Paris: Laffont (Coll. 'Vécu'), 1975, pp.45–58.

Bb1396   Rosolato, Guy, '*L'Amour fou*', in *Du surréalisme et du plaisir* [see Bb981], pp.125–36.

Bb1397   ——, Ref. in *Psychanalyse et musique*, Paris: Les Belles Lettres (Coll. 'Confluents psychanalytiques'), 1982, pp.153–55.

Bb1398   Rossani, Wolfango, 'Posizione di AB', in *Patriarchi del novecento*, Milan: Pan, 1974, pp.49–58.

Bb1399   Roudaut, Jean, 'L'Amour fatal', *Le Magazine littéraire*, 213 (déc.84), 32–34.

Bb1400   ——, 'Le Hasard objectif comme providence', in Ba67, pp.46–47.

Bb1401   Roudiez, Leon S., CR of Ba8, *Romanic Review*, LXV, 2 (March 74), 142–44.

Bb1402   Roudinesco, Elisabeth, 'L'Autre de la théorie', *Action poétique*, 53 (1973), 1–7.*

Bb1403   Rougemont, Denis de, Refs in 'Quelques-uns de mes écrivains', in *De l'ordre et de l'aventure. Mélanges offerts à Pierre Olivier Walzer*, Neuchâtel: La Baconnière (Coll. 'Langages'), 1985, pp.187–93 ('AB à New York', pp.190–92).

Bb1404   Rousset, Jean. *Leurs yeux se rencontrèrent. La scène de première vue dans le roman*, Paris: Corti, 1981, pp.27–29, 90.

Bb1405   Roy, Claude, 'L'Anarchiste parfait', *Le Nouvel observateur*, 1228 (20–26 mai 88), 59–61.

Bb1406   ——, 'Passage d'AB', and 'AB, juste un profil', in *Somme toute*, Paris: Gallimard, 1976, pp.267–300 and 405–19.

Bb1407   Roy, Claude, 'La Profanation de l'art' [CR of Ba46], *Le Nouvel observateur*, 562 (18–24 aout 75), 44–46.

Bb1408   Rubes, Jan, 'La Correspondance pragoise: histoire et jalons en marge du surréalisme', *Courrier du Centre International d'Études Poétiques* (Brussels), 123–8 (nov.–déc.78), 5–15. Contains extracts of letters between AB and Nezval, from Museum of Czech Literature, Prague.

Bb1409   ——, 'Nezval a Breton (Zamyslení nad korespondencí mezi českými a francouzskými surrealisty)' [Nezval and Breton (Thoughts on a correspondence between Czech and French Surrealists)], *Časopis pro Moderní Filologii* (Prague), 61 (1979), 17–21.

Bb1410   Saint-Exupéry, Antoine de, Refs in *Carnets*, Paris: Gallimard, 1975, pp.52, 75, 93, 112, 134.

Bb1411   ——, Letter to AB (1941), *Cahiers Saint-Exupéry*, 3 (1989).*

Bb1412   Salmon, André, Refs in *Souvenirs sans fin*, Vol. 3 (1920–40): Gallimard, 1961, pp.51–57, 60–64, 69, 81–82, 383.*

Bb1413   Saporta, Marc, 'L'Épisode américain', in Ba87, pp.33–35.

Bb1414   ——, 'Les Surréalistes sont parmi nous', in Ba87, pp.9–11.

Bb1415   Sarkany, Stéphane, '*Nadja* ou la lecture du monde objectif', *Mélusine*, 4 (1982), 101–09.

Bb1416   Scalia, Gianni, 'Poesia, politica: Défense de toucher', in Ba38, pp.89–120.

Bb1417   Schabert, Tilo, Refs in *Gewalt und Humanität. Über philosophische und politische Manifestationen von Modernität*, Freiburg, Munich: Karl Alber, 1978, pp.22, 292–97, 307, 319.

Bb1418   Scharfman, Ronnie, 'Reading Breton Today: "La Mort Rose"', in Ba53, pp.67–73.

Bb1419   Scherer, Thomas M., Refs in *Textanalytische Studien zur 'l'écriture automatique'*, Bonn: Romanisches Seminar der Universität, 1974.*

Bb1420   Schmelz, Gabrielle, 'Bretons "Köstliche Leiche" — Notizen zu einem Schreibspiel', *Deutschunterricht*, 4 (1980), 90–101.*

Bb1421   Schneider, Marcel, 'AB, mystique de la poésie', *Le Figaro littéraire*, 13632 (27 juin 88), III, 31.

Bb1422   Schoenfeld, Jean Snitzer, 'AB, Alchemist', *French Review*, LVII, 4 (March 84), 493–502.

Bb1423   ——, 'AB and the Poet/Reader', *Dada/Surrealism*, 13 (1984), 115–22.

Bb1424   Schuster, Jean, '17 sans 13', in Ba87, pp.36–43; also in *Les Fruits de la passion*, Paris: L'instant (Coll. 'Griffures'), pp.9–29.

Bb1425   ——, 'Sommeil d'or', in Ba66, pp.22–24; also in *Les Fruits de la passion* [see Bb1424], pp.133–53.

        ——, see Bb1184.

Bb1426   Schwarz, Arturo, 'Anarchie, alchimie, tantrisme et surréalisme', *L'Arc*, 91–92 (1984), 38–43.

Bb1427   ——, 'AB e Leone Trotskij', in *Studi sul surrealismo* [see Bb889], pp.433–71. Extract from Ba89.

Bb1428   ——, & Maurice Nadeau, Letters (17 oct.75), *Les Lettres nouvelles*, 5 (déc.75), 189–91.

Bb1429   Scutenaire, Louis, 'Témoignages', in Ba74, pp.22–23.

Bb1429a   Sebbag, Georges, Refs in *L'Imprononçable Jour de sa mort Jacques Vaché janvier 1919*, Paris: Jean-Michel Place, 1989, *passim*. Includes a collage by AB (see Ac849).

Bb1430   Sellin, Eric, 'Simultaneity: Driving Force of the Surrealist Aesthetic', *Twentieth Century Literature*, XXI, 1 (Feb.75), 10–23.

Bb1431   ——, CR of Ba4, *Romanic Review*, LXIV, 4 (Nov.73), 316–19.

Bb1432   Sheringham, Michael, 'Breton and the Language of Automatism: Alterity, Allegory, Desire', in *Surrealism and Language* [see Bb1095], pp.142–58.

Bb1433   ——, 'Le Film des durées' [CR of Ba89], *La Chouette*, 21 (mars 89), 25–30.

Bb1434   ——, 'From the Labyrinth of Language to the Language of the Senses', in Roger Cardinal, ed., *Sensibility and Creation: Studies in Twentieth Century French Poetry*, London: Croom Helm, New York: Barnes & Noble, 1977, pp.72–102.

Bb1435   ——, 'The Liberator of Desire' [CR of Aa839], *TLS*, 4462 (7–13 oct.88), 1125.

Bb1436   ——, '*Mont de piété* and AB's Early Poetic Development', *Forum for Modern Language Studies*, XV, 1 (Jan.79), 46–68.

Bb1437   ——, 'Rimbaud in 1875 and AB's "Forêt-Noire"', *French Studies*, XXXV, 1 (Jan.81), 32–44.

Bb1438   ——, CR of Ba45, *Modern Language Review*, LXXVIII, 3 (July 78), 651–52.

Bb1439   Sheringham, Michael, CR of Ba91, *ibid.*, XXXVIII, 3 (July 84), 367–68.

Bb1440   Siepe, Hans T., 'Traum-Analyse: ein Traum Bretons' and 'Bretons "poème-objet"', in *Der Leser des Surrealismus. Untersuchungen zur Kommunikationsästhetik*, Stuttgart: Klett-Cotta, 1977, pp.134–36 and 213–19.

Ba1441   Simonis, Ippolito, 'AB e la nozione di "humour"', in Ba38, pp.121–35.

Bb1442   Simpkins, Scott, 'Surrealism and Breton's "Textes solubles". An Index to Modernism', *Comparative Literature Studies*, XXV, 3 (1988), 242–50.

Bb1443   Smith, Susan Harris, 'Breton's "Femme et oiseau": An Interpretation', *Dada/Surrealism*, 6 (1976), 37–39.

Bb1444   Sojcher, Jacques, Refs in *La Démarche poétique*, Paris: UGE (Coll. '10/18'), 1976, pp.52–56.

Bb1445   Sollers, Philippe, 'Breton manifeste', *Le Monde [des livres]*, 13470 (20 mai 88), 1, 22; also in 'Journal du joueur II', *L'Infini*, 23 (aut.88), 53–56.

Bb1446   Somville, Léon, 'Pour une théorie des débuts. Une analyse de l'incipit de l'œuvre d'AB', in *Le Surréalisme dans le texte* [see Bb856], pp.41–57.

Bb1447   Soupault, Philippe, 'AB', in Ba38, pp.170–72.

Bb1448   ——, 'Le Chef d'école cachait un solitaire' (interview with Bruno De Cessole), *Le Figaro littéraire*, 13632 (27 juin 88), 33.

Bb1449   ——, Refs in *Vingt mille et un jours. Entretiens avec Serge Fauchereau*, Paris: Belfond, 1980 (see index).

Bb1450   Spada, Marcel, 'Gustave Moreau et l'Eve nouvelle d'AB', in Philippe Bonnefis, Pierre Reboul, eds., *Des mots et des couleurs. Études sur le rapport de la littérature et de la peinture (XIXe et XXe siècles)*, Lille: Presses Universitaires de Lille, 1979, pp.145-63.

Bb1451   Spatola, Adriano, 'Scrittura come collaborazione', in Ba38, pp.136-43.

Bb1452   Speranza Armani, Ada, 'Breton e Valéry: tempo di ricerca', in *Surréalisme-Surrealismo* [see Bb1016], pp.223-38.

Bb1453   Spies, Werner, Refs in *Max Ernst — Collagen. Inventar und Widerspruch*, Cologne: M. DuMont Schauberg, 1974, *passim*; also tr. under title *Max Ernst. Les Collages. Inventaire et contradictions*, tr. Eliane Kaufholz, Paris: Gallimard, 1984.

Bb1454   Stalloni, Yves, 'Pour une Lecture de *Nadja* comme introduction au surréalisme', *L'École des lettres*, LXXIV, 11 (15 mars 83), 3-16.

Bb1455   Stamelman, Richard, 'AB and the Poetry of Intimate Presence', *Dada/Surrealism*, 5 (1975), 58-65.

Bb1456   ——, The Relational Structure of Surrealist Poetry', *Dada/Surrealism*, 6 (1976), 59-78.

Bb1457   ——, 'Surrealist Poetry: The Revolt against Mimesis', *Kentucky Romance Quarterly*, XXII, 4 (1975), 561-71.

Bb1458   Steel, David A., 'Autour d'un poème de jeunesse d'AB: "Pour Lafcadio"', *Théorie, tableau, texte, Le Siècle éclaté*, 2 (1978), 141-49.

Bb1459   Steinmetz, Jean-Luc, 'Du sarcasme à l'émerveillement. Un carré de lecteurs: Baudelaire, Ducasse, Jammes, Breton', *Revue d'histoire littéraire de la France*, LXXXIX, 5 (sept.–oct.89), 910–22.

Bb1460   ——, 'Le Surréalisme interdit', in Ba83, pp.33–58.

Bb1461   Stoll, André, 'Beatrice im Versteck. Zu Bretons surrealistischer Revolution: *Nadja*', *Merkur*, XXXVIII, 4 (Juni 84), 380–91.

Bb1462   Suleiman, Susan R., 'Nadja, Dora, Lol V.Stein: Women, Madness and Narrative', in S. Rimmon-Kenan, ed., *Discourse in Psychoanalysis and Literature*, London: Methuen, 1987.*

Bb1463   Tabart, Claude-André, 'AB: *Clair de terre*', *L'École des lettres*, LXXIV, 11 (15 mars 83), 17–23.

Bb1464   ——, 'AB: "Nœud des miroirs"', *ibid.*, LXXVI, 10 (1 mars 85), 21–26.

Bb1465   Tadié, Jean-Yves, Refs in *Le Récit poétique*, Paris: PUF (Coll. 'Ecriture'), 1978, *passim*.

Bb1466   Tamuly, Annette, 'AB et la notion d'équivoque', *Mélusine*, 5, (1983), 195–207.

Bb1467   Taracido, Susan L., 'Breton: A Poetry of Sensual Union', *Publications of the Missouri Philological Association*, 7 (1982), 43–47.*

Bb1468   Terrasse, Jean, 'Les manifestes surréalistes', in *Rhétorique de l'essai littéraire*, Montréal: Presses de l'Université du Quebec, 1977, p.87–101.

Bb1469   Thévenin, Paule, 'A Marseille l'imagination n'était pas au rendez-vous', *La Quinzaine littéraire*, 465 (16–30 juin 86), 17.

Bb1470 Thiercelin-Mejias, Raquel, 'El Reflejo de "Nadja" en los espejos valados: (Una fuente surrealista en "El Hacedor" de J.L. Borges)', *Cuadernos hispanoamericanos*, 372 (junio 81), 620–32.

Bb1471 Thirion, André, 'AB', in *Révolutionnaires sans révolution*, Paris: Laffont, 1972, 1988, pp.192–220; also tr. under title *Revolutionaries without Revolution*, tr. Joachim Neugroschel, London: Cassell, 1975, pp.172–99.

Bb1472 Tison Braun, Micheline, 'AB et la topographie de l'imaginaire', *Symposium*, XLII, 3 (Fall 88), 246–60.

Bb1473 ——, 'Scientist and Poet: Two Views of Chance', *Dada/Surrealism*, 7 (1977), 66–75.

Bb1474 Tola, Luigi, 'AB: Per una letteratura dell'impazienza e dell'insoddisfazione', in Ba38, pp.173–75.

Bb1475 Tran Van Khai, Michelle, 'Flagrant hasard, déflagrations du plaisir', in *Du surréalisme et du plaisir* [see Bb981], pp.111–24.

Bb1476 Tremaine, Louis, 'Breton's *Nadja*: A Spiritual Ethnography', *Studies in Twentieth Century Literature*, I, 1 (Fall 76), 91–119.*

Bb1477 Trotsky, Leon, Bb749, also in *Writings of Leon Trotsky*, New York: Pathfinder Press, 1974, p.93.*

Bb1478 Tytell, Pamela, 'Freud contre Breton', in *La Plume sur le divan. Psychanalyse et littérature en France*, Paris: Aubier Montaigne 1982, pp.36–41.

Bb1479 Ungar, Steven, 'Sartre, Breton and Black Orpheus: Vicissitudes of Poetry and Politics', *L'Ésprit créateur*, XVII, 1 (Spring 77), 3–18.

Bb1480　　Vaché, Jacques, Bb751, also in Arthur Cravan, Jacques Rigaut, Jacques Vaché, *Trois suicidés de la société*, Paris: Eric Losfeld/UGE (Coll. '10/18'), 1974.

Bb1481　　Valle, Rafael H., 'Dialogues with AB', *Transformaction* (Devon), 6 (1973), 6–11.*

Bb1482　　Velazquez, J.Ignacio, 'Breton y su "double sombre": Nadja', *Atlantis. A Woman's Studies Journal* (Fall 87), 425–37*; also in Jesús García Gallego, ed., *Surrealismo. El ojo soluble*, Málaga: Litoral, 1987.

Bb1483　　Veseley, Dalibor, 'Surrealism, Myth and Modernity', *Architectural Design*, XLVIII, 2–3 (1978), 87–95.

Bb1484　　Vermeersch, P., 'AB et la recherche du tychique dans *Les Vases communicants*', *Psychologie médicale*, XIV, 9 (1982), 1373–79.

Bb1485　　Vier, Jacques, 'A propos de *Nadja* d'AB. Occultisme et désinvolture', *Points et contrepoints*, 113 (déc.74), 65–68; also in *Figures de proue et magots de brocante. Études de littérature moderne et contemporaine*, Paris: Nouvelles Éditions Latines, 1978, pp.181–86.

Bb1486　　Vincent, Mora, 'ABs *Nadja*: Struktur-och meningsanalys av en surrealistisk roman'[AB's *Nadja*: structural and semantic analysis of a Surrealist novel], *Samlaren* (Uppsala), 102 (1981), 26–36.*

Bb1487　　Violato, Gabriella, 'Per una lettura di *Nadja*', in *Lo scarto e la norma. Studi sul surrealismo*, Rome: n.d., pp.7–49.*

Bb1488　　Virmaux, Alain and Odette, 'Le cinéma: un autre "bilan d'infortune". La part d'AB', in Ba87, pp.87–98.

Bb1489   Vital Le Bossé, Michel, '"Le merveilleux spirite", ésotérisme et poésie, psychanalyse, parapsychologie: l'expérience surréaliste', in Ba74, pp.57–77.

Bb1490   Vogt, Ulrich, '*Au lavoir noir* ou du mythique dans le texte surréaliste', in *L'Objet au défi* [see Bb981], pp.21–37.

Bb1491   ——, 'Osiris anarchiste. Le miroir noir du surréalisme', *Mélusine*, 5 (1983), 142–58.

Bb1492   Volker, Eckhard, 'Philosophische Erkenntnis und Sinneserfahrung in Aragons *Paysan de Paris* und Bretons *Poisson soluble*', *Lendemains*, III, 9 (Jan.78), 49–61.

Bb1493   Vollé, Jean-Paul, 'Breton et Freud', *Le Magazine littéraire*, 213 (déc.84), 35.

Bb1494   Wachsmann, Paul, 'L'Universalité d'AB', *L'Orne littéraire*, 11 (1987), 54–59.

Bb1495   Wagner, Nicolas, 'Nadja, ville de l'angoisse', in *Travaux de linguistique et de littérature* (Strasbourg), XIV, 2 (1976), 221–28.

Bb1496   Waite, Alan, 'Sens et absence dans *Nadja*', *Romanic Review*, LXXVII, 3 (nov.86), 376–90.

Bb1497   Waldberg, Patrick, Refs in *Yves Tanguy*, Brussels: André de Rache, 1972 (see index). Contains extract of letter from AB to Emilie Tanguy.

Bb1498   Warehime, Marja, 'Beginning and Ending: The Utility of Dreams in *Les Vases communicants*', *French Forum*, VI, 2 (May 81), 163–71.

Bb1499 Warren, Barrett, 'Method and Surrealism: The Politics of Poetry', *Open Letter*, VI, 1 (Winter 82), 129–40.

Bb1500 Wayne, Eric, 'Narrative Structure and the Surrealist Poem', *Dada/Surrealism*, 8 (1978), 115–23.

Bb1501 Wetzel, Hermann H., 'Zur Analyse und Deutung surrealistischer Werke (A.Breton)', *Degré second*, 2 (June 78), 137–74.

Bb1502 Winston, Mathew, 'Humour noir and black humor', in Harry Levin, *Veins of Humor*, Cambridge: Harvard U.P., 1972, pp.269–84.*

Bb1503 York, R.A., 'Intersentence Connections in Two Surrealist Texts', *Neophilologus*, LXIV, 1 (Jan.80), 19–31.

Bb1504 Young, Alan, 'What is Surrealism?', in *Dada and After. Extremist Modernism and English Literature*, Manchester: Manchester U.P., New Jersey: Humanities Press, 1981, pp.110–26.

Bb1505 Zima, Pierre, 'Objet trouvé/sujet perdu', *Les Lettres nouvelles*, 4 (sept.–oct.72), 153–74.

Bb1506 Zivadin, Steven, 'Techniques in Surrealist Poetry', *Pennine Platform* (West Yorks.) II, 3 (1976), 8–11.*

Bb1507 Zoppi, Sergio, Refs in *Al festino di Esopo*, Roma: Bulzoni Editore, 1979 (see index).

Bb1508 Zuern, John, 'The Communicating Labyrinth: Breton's "La Maison d'Yves" as a Micro-*Manifeste*', in Ba53, pp.111–20.

c. Theses

Bc1600 Acker Jole, Jocelyne, 'Analyse des structures sémantiques et sémiotiques de *L'Ode à Charles Fourier* de Breton', Thèse de 3e cycle, Strasbourg II, 1975, 164pp.*

Bc1601 Adamowicz Dunwoodie, Elza, 'A Stammering Staircase: Association and Disruption in AB's Surrealist Poetry (1919–1939)', PhD, London, 1985, 270pp.

Bc1602 Ariew, Robert Abel, 'La Thématique du *Poisson soluble*: étude cybernétique', PhD, Illinois, 1974, 131pp. [Diss.Abst., 36, 2, 920–A]*

Bc1603 Asari, Makoto, 'AB et le sacré: essai sur Breton selon quelques thèmes religieux', Thèse de 3e cycle, Paris III, 1985.*

Bc1603 Aspley, Keith R., 'The Poetry and Poetic Theory of AB, with Particular Reference to the Image', PhD, Edinburgh, 1975.

Bc1604 Babonneau, Marie-José, 'La Femme souveraine dans l'œuvre de Chrétien de Troyes et d'AB', Thèse de 3e cycle, Nice, 1979.*

Bc1605 Ballabriga, Miche, 'Etude sémio-linguistique du discours surréaliste (AB): construction d'une cohérence', Thèse d'État, Paris, 1988, 722pp.

Bc1606 Batache, Eddy, 'Recherches sur les affinités et les divergences dans la pensée d'AB et René Guénon', Thèse de 3e cycle, 1977.*

Bc1607 Beauchard-Colombo, Marie-Joseph, 'La Tension utopique chez Tristan Tzara et AB', Thèse de 3e cycle, Paris III, 1986.*

Bc1608 Blachère, Jean-Claude, 'AB et les mondes primitifs', Thèse d'État, Paris IV, 1986.*

Bc1609 Bonnet, Marguerite, 'AB. Naissance de l'aventure surréaliste', Thèse d'État, Paris IV, 1975.

Bc1610   Bonnet, Marguerite, 'AB: *Mont de piété* et *Alentours* 1913–1919. Édition critique', Thèse complémentaire, Paris IV, 1975, 108pp.

Bc1611   Burke, Mary Ann, 'The *Merveilleux* as a Category of Esthetic Expression in a Selection of Medieval Works and in the Surrealist Novels of AB and Louis Aragon', PhD, Wisconsin, 1974, 277pp. [Diss.Abst., 35, 7, 4502–A]*

Bc1612   Coppay, Francis L., 'Le Récit minimal', PhD, Univ. of Wisconsin, 1981, 359pp. [Diss.Abst., 42, 8 (Feb.82), 3622–A]*

Bc1613   Crespi, Marcantonio, '*Nadja* et *L'Amour fou*: les textes communicants d'AB', PhD, Rutgers, 1987, 200pp. [Diss.Abst., 48, 7 (Jan.88), 1786–7A]*

Bc1614   Danier, Richard, 'L'Hermétisme alchimique chez AB. Interprétation de la symbolique de trois œuvres du poète', Thèse de 3e cycle, Paris X, 1973.*

Bc1615   Dazut, Mireille, 'Contribution à une édition critique de *La Clé des champs*', Thèse de 3e cycle, Tours, 1981, 340pp.*

Bc1616   Dickinson, Richard Taliaferro, 'The Animal Metamorphoses of AB', PhD, New York Univ., 1983, 322pp. [Diss.Abst., 44, 2 (Aug.83), 481–A]*

Bc1617   Duda, Clairette, 'Les Collages dans les œuvres poétiques et autobiographiques de Breton', Thèse de 3e cycle, Nice, 1975, 2 vols, 173pp and 178pp.*

Bc1618   Ellenwood, William, 'AB and Freud', PhD, Rutgers, 1972, 273pp. [Diss.Abst., 33, 7 (Jan.73) 4340–A]*

Bc1619   Fauchet, Catherine, 'L'Alchimie du quotidien chez le surréaliste AB', Thèse de 3e cycle, Paris IV, 1983.*

Bc1620   Finck, Jeanine, 'Tentatives mystiques de trois poètes incroyants (1924–1940): Breton, Daumal, Bousquet (1920–1940)', Thèse de 3e cycle, Paris VIII, 1975, 229pp.

Bc1621   Follet, Jeanne, 'La Poésie d'AB à la lumière du *Manifeste du surréalisme*', Thèse de 3e cycle, Lille III, 1979.*

Bc1622   Gabellone, Pasquale, 'Situation de l'objet dans l'œuvre d'AB (pour une archéologie du surréalisme)', Thèse DU, Montpellier III, 1976, 150pp.*

Bc1623   Gernant, Mary Kathleen, 'Movement, Rest and Metamorphosis: An Essay on the Poetics of AB', PhD, North Carolina, 1979, 206pp. [Diss.Abst., 40, 6 (Dec.79), 3340-A]*

Bc1624   Gibs, Barbara, 'Analyse du récit surréaliste (*Nadja, Etes-vous fou?, Au château d'Argol*)', Thèse de 3e cycle, Paris VII, 1974, 187pp.*

Bc1625   Gouret, Monique, 'Aspects de la figure féminine dans *Arcane 17* d'AB: ésotérisme et révolution', Thèse de 3e cycle, Rennes II, 1981.*

Bc1626   Graff, Marc, 'Pensée poétique et pensée mythique dans *Arcane 17* (AB)', Thèse de 3e cycle, Paris VIII, 1984.*

Bc1627   Gratton, Johnnie, 'The Poetic Language of AB', PhD, Univ. of Kent, Canterbury, 1981.

Bc1628   Green, Leslie Anne, 'Mythes et archétypes dans une œuvre surréaliste: *Poisson soluble* d'AB', PhD, Northwestern Univ., 1980, 226pp. [Diss.Abst., 41, 9 (Mar 81), 4054-A]*

Bc1629   Hanson, Marja Warehime, 'Paradox and Contradiction: AB's Problems in Defining Surrealism', PhD, Johns Hopkins, 1975, 195pp. [Diss.Abst., 36, 7 (Jan.76), 4540-A]*

Bc1630   Hudson, Janette Caton, 'Achim von Armin und AB: Zur Verwandtschaft der deutschen Romantik und des französischen Surrealismus', PhD, Illinois, 1973, 314pp. [Diss.Abst., 34, 9 (Dec.73), 5972-A]*

Bc1631   Lamy, Suzanne, 'L'Ecriture convulsive d'"Arcane 17", discours, intertextualité, polysémie', PhD, Montréal, 1976, 556pp.*

Bc1632   Lang, Carol Elizabeth, 'The Surrealist Novel: Its Principles and Structures in AB's *Nadja*, *Amour fou*, and *Arcane 17*', PhD, Arizona, 1980, 279pp. [Diss.Abst., 41, 10 (Apr.81), 4413-A]*

Bc1633   Le Gros, Marc, 'Les Figures du changement de signe dans *Arcane 17* d'AB', Thèse de 3e cycle, Brest, 1980.*

Bc1634   Matsuur, Hisaki, 'AB et la topologie du texte', Thèse de 3e cycle, Paris III, 1981.*

Bc1635   Metzidakis, Stamos, 'Repetition and Semiotics: Reading Prose Poems' [Baudelaire, Rimbaud and AB], PhD, Columbia, 1982, 177pp. [Diss.Abst., 45, 10 (Apr.85), 3141-A]*

Bc1636   Migeot, François, 'AB et le discours freudien dans *Les Vases communicants*', Thèse de 3e cycle, Paris VIII, 1981.*

Bc1637   Mor, Samuel, 'An Inquiry into Madness: The Meaning of Madness in the Works of Virginia Woolf, AB, and Y.H. Brenner', PhD, South California, 1979. [Diss.Abst., 40, 4 (Oct.79), 2049-A]*

Bc1638   Novel, Martin, 'The Unconscious in Freud and Breton', PhD, Waterloo (Canada), 1973. [Diss.Abst., 34, 10 (Apr.74), 6703-A]*

Bc1639   Oh, Saeng-Keung, 'Les Récits d'AB: *Nadja, Les Vases communicants, L'Amour fou*: formes et signification', Thèse de 3e cycle, Paris X, 1983.*

Bc1640   Parmentier, Michel Alfred, 'De l'aliénation à l'intégration dans la pensée d'AB: la relation à soi, à la femme, à la communauté humaine et au monde', PhD, Toronto, 1977. [Diss.Abst. 39, 7 (Jan.79), 4247-8A]*

Bc1641   Pierre, José, alias Darrambide, 'AB et la peinture', Thèse d'État, Paris IV, 1980.

Bc1642   Queilles, Gérard, 'AB et G. Bataille: dépassement et absolu ou le rapport à Hegel', Thèse de 3e cycle, Paris IV, 1978.*

Bc1643   Ramet, Robert David, 'The Interrelation of Politics and Poetry as Seen in the Works of AB and Pablo Neruda', PhD, Berkeley, 1976, 430pp. [Diss.Abst., 38, 2 (Aug.77). 776-A]*

Bc1644   Saliou, Jean, 'La Pensée surréaliste et le continuum spatio-temporel à travers les textes fondamentaux d'AB', Thèse de 3e cycle, Paris III, 1978, 287pp.*

Bc1645   Sayegh, Alia, 'The Concept and Role of Woman in the Works of AB', PhD, Pennsylvania, 1975, 254pp. [Diss.Abst., 36, 1 (July 75), 328-9-A]*

Bc1646   Stultz, Janice Elaine, '*Poisson soluble*, the Poetic Quest of AB', PhD, Princeton, 1977, 579pp. [Diss.Abst., 38, 3 (Sept.77), 1443-A]*

INDEX

References to publications as catalogued in first volume are given in brackets where appropriate

'Bas les masques, Bas les pattes!'
[Ad503], Ad502a, Ac804, Ac815
'Baya' [Ab386], Ab834
'Bocaux Dada' [Ab47], Ac786, Aa839
'Le Bouquet sans fleurs' [Ab114],
Ac766, Aa839
'Boussole', Ad656a, Ac804
'Braise au trépied de Keridwen'
[Ac574], Ac802
[Brauner], Ad421a, A804
'Brique de cinamome', Aa839
Bureau de recherches surréalistes...,
Ad842

'Ça commence bien!' [Ad548], Ad830
'Un Cadavre', Ad111d, Ac797
'Le Cadavre exquis, son exaltation'
[Ac418], Ac765
'Camaïeu', Aa795.1, Aa839
'Camarades, plus de lumière...'
[Ad287], Ac779, Ac797
'Carnet' [101.1], Aa839
'Carnet' (1920–1921), Aa839
'Carte postale' [Ab316.1], Ac794
'Carte postale au Général Gouraud',
Ac797.4
'Ce grain de merveilleux...' [Ab416],
Ab812
'Ce que pensent, ce que veulent les
surréalistes' [A481b], Ac804
'Ce que Tanguy voile et dévoile'
[Ac331], Ac806
'Certifiés sans la moindre retouche...',
Ab768.1
'C'est toi ce n'est pas nous...', Aa839
'C'est un rosier...', Aa839
'Ceux dont on ne parle pas...' [Ab97],
Aa839
Les Champs magnétiques [Aa29],
Aa839, Aa844
'Chansons internationales', Aa839
'Le Chapelet des aiguilles', Aa839
'Chaumont...', Ac439.3, Aa839

'Le Cinquantenaire de l'hystérie'
[Ab158], Ac766, Ac797, Aa839
Clair de terre [Aa85], Aa839
'Clairement' [Ab73], Ac786
La Claire Tour [Ab485], Aa745, Ac779,
Ac815
'*Clarté, Philosophies, La Révolution
surréaliste* solidaires du Comité
Central d'Action. Aux soldats et
aux marins', Ad127a, Ac797
La Clé des champs [Aa506], Aa754
'Clé de sol' [Ab17], Ac230a, Ac786
'Clôture définitive des affaires
Carrouges et Pastoureau', Ac804.1
'Comme il fait beau' [Ab87], Ac786,
Aa839
'Comme une châsse d'or...', Aa839
'Concours de circonstances', Aa839
'Contre-attaque—Sous le feu...'
[Ad267], Ac797
'Contre-attaque: Union de lutte...'
[Ad254], Ac797
'Contre le fascisme mais aussi contre
l'impérialisme français', Ad215c.
'Contre vents et marées...', Ab584a,
Ac779
'Coqs de bruyère' [Ab2], Ac799, Aa839
'Coquito', Aa839
'Correspondance' [Ab204], Ac774
'Le Corset mystère' [Ab20], Ac230a,
Ac717a, Ac786
'Costume-tailleur', Ab809.1, Aa804
'Cote d'alerte' [Ad576], Ac804
'Couleur d'heure', Aa839
'Coup de semonce' [Ad592], Ac804
'Cours-les toutes', Aa406.3
'Cycle systématique de conférences...'
[Ad249], Ac797

'Dada n'est pas mort' [Ab54], Ac786
'De fil en aiguille', Ab809.2, Aa804
De la jurisprudence surréaliste, Ad751
De la survivance de certains mythes...,
Aa845

143

'Le Masque du jour', Aa839
'Masques à transformation de la côte
    Pacifique du Nord-Ouest', Ab455a,
    Ab821
[Matta], Ad421a, Ac804
'Max Ernst' [Ac56], Ac61a, Aa839
'La Médecine mentale devant le
    surréalisme' [Ab182], Ac774
'Mes pas dans les tiens...', Aa839
'Message des surréalistes aux
    intellectuels polonais', Ad628b,
    Ac804
'Mise au point de notre camarade AB'
    [Ab491], Ac779, Ac815
'Mise en accusation d'Arthur Meyer',
    Aa839
'Misère de la poésie: "L'Affaire
    Aragon"...' [Aa197], Ac797
'La Mobilisation contre la guerre n'est
    pas la paix' [Ad26], Ac797
'Monsieur V' [Aa15.2], Ab16b, Aa839
'Motion adressée au Juge Perez',
    Ad591a
'Les Mots sans rides' [Ab78], Ac786
'Un Mouchoir noir...', Aa839

Nadja [Aa683], Aa747, Aa839
'Neutralité? Non-sens, crime et
    trahison!' [Ad272], Ac797
'Ne visitez pas l'exposition coloniale'
    [Ad192], Ac721a, Ac797
'Ni aujourd'hui ni de cette manière',
    Ad708b, Ac768, Ac779
'Ni de votre guerre ni de votre paix!'
    [Ad299], Ac797
'N'imitez pas Hitler!' [Ad312], Ac797
'Note' [Ab18], Ac786, Aa839
Note: on Freud [Ab291], Ac797; on
    Péret [Ac349], Ac804
'Notes sur la poésie' [Ab168], Ac766,
    Ab822, Aa839
'Notice': for Prassinos, *Le Feu
    maniaque*, Ac358a, Aa447

'Les Oiseaux de menuisier vers le
    pôle...' [Ab37.1], Ac631b
'On s'est avisé...'[from Aa99.2], Ab11a
'Opinions — AB' [Ac123], Aa839
'Où en est le surréalisme?', Ab763
'Ouvrez les prisons, licenciez l'armée'
    [Ad124], Ac766
'Ouvrez-vous?', Ab768.2

'Les Pages marquées de craie...',
    Ab823, Aa839
'La Paix par nous-mêmes', Ad421b
*Paravent pour les douze mois de
    l'année*, Ac723a
'Parfums d'Orsay' [Ab44], Aa839
'Par le froid...', Aa839
'Pas de patrie' [Ad311], Ac797
Les Pas perdus [Aa98], Aa839
'Patinage Dada' [Ab48], Ac786
'Paul Eluard', Aa839
'La Peinture: Michel G. Vivancos'
    [Ac460], Ab453a, Ac815
'Permettez' [Ad151], Ac797
'Philippe Soupault' [Ab91], Ac786
    Aa839
'Le Pinceau de l'amour', Ac757, Aa839
'La Planète sans visa' [Ad234], Ac721a,
    Ac779
'Plutôt la vie' [Aa85.7], Ab97b
'Poème avec vocabulaire', Ac758.3
'Poème destiné à être lu au mariage de
    T. Fraenkel', Aa839
'Poème exhibitionniste', Ac758.4
'Poème fin du monde', Ac758.5
'Poèmes' [Ab134], Ac766
'Poèmes' [Ab86], Ac786
Poisson soluble [II], Aa839
'La porte de la maison de Lise...',
    Aa839
'Portrait étrange', Aa839
'Portrait: Madame Marie Laurencin'
    [Ab5], Aa839
'Postface[s]': Oleg Ibrahimoff, *Le
    Prince Oleg et autres dits*, Ac770;

Ad127f, Ac721a, Ac766, Ac794, Ac797
'Revues' [Ab23], Ac786
'Rieuse' [Ab1.2], Aa795, Aa839
'Riposte. La Bénédiction de l'un vaut l'autopsie de l'autre', Ad627b.1, Ac804
'Ris, poste...', Aa839
'Robert Desnos', Ab101a, Aa839
'Rondel', Aa839
'Le Rouge est assez aéré...', Aa839
'Roulades...', Aa839
'La Rupture avec *Contre-attaque*', Ad267a, Ac797
'Rupture inaugurale' [Ad398], Ac804

'Saludo a Tenerife', Ab236a.
'Sans cérémonie...', Aa839
'Sauve qui peut' [Ad642], Ac804
'Saxe fin' Le [Ab1.1], Aa795, Aa839
Second manifeste du surréalisme [Aa175], Aa174a, Aa839
'Second manifeste du surréalisme' [Ab167], Ac766
'Silence is Golden' [Ab379], Ab755
'Si le surréalisme était maître de Paris' [Ab467], Ac804, Ac807
'S'il vous plaît' [Ab53], Ac786, Aa839
'Situation de Melmoth' [Ac547], Ac846
'Soldat', Aa839
'Le soleil est un chien basset...' Ac758.1, Aa839
'La Somnambule' [Ac601], Ac804
'Souvenir du Mexique' [Ab309], Ac779
'Suite princière' [Ad630], Ac804
'Sujet' [Ab7], Ac799, Aa839
'Les supplices paresseux...', Aa839
'Sur Robert Desnos' [Aa726.3], Ac839
'Le Surréalisme et la peinture' [Aa154], Ac766
'Surrealistas y anarquistas' [Ad481a], Ad482b, Ac779
'Les Surréalistes à Garry Davis' [Ad440], Ac804

'Les surréalistes: "Les fascistes sont ceux qui tirent sur le peuple"', Ad577b, Ac804
'Sus au misérabilisme!' [Ab566], Ac804

'La taillerie de diamants...', Aa839
'Tapis lisible', Aa839
'Télégramme au Président du Conseil de Hongrie', Ad127b, Ad711a, Ac797.
'Terre de couleur' [Ab41], Ac631b
'Texte adressé à 99 intellectuels français (10 avril 59)', Ad620a, Ac804
'Texte de Breton écrit pour la *Literaturnaja Gazeta* à la demande de Romoff', Ab762
'Textes surréalistes' [Ab131], Ac766
'Thomas de Quincey (1784–1859)' [from Aa315], Ab368a, Ac794
'Tir de barrage' [Ad628], Ac804
'Titre' [Ab58], Aa839
'Les toits de briques...', Aa839
'Tout va bien' [Ab187.2], Ac774
'Toutes les écolières ensemble'[Aa195.7], Ab176a
'Tranchons-en', Ac804.8
'Treize études' [Ab8], Aa839
'Trente ans après' [Ab413], Ac760
'Le 31 juillet 1958. Poésie 58. AB' [Bb194], Ab773
'Le Trésor des jésuites' [Ab165], Aa839
'Le "Troisième degré" de la peinture', Ad699a, Ac804
'Tu es grave...', Aa839
'Tu n'es pas...', Aa839

'L'Union libre' [Aa186], Ac230a
'Usine' [Ab21], Ac786

'Vacances d'artiste' [Ab76], Ac786, Aa839
'Le Verbe être' [Aa195.4], Ab176a, Ac230a

RESEARCH BIBLIOGRAPHIES AND CHECKLISTS
Edited by
A.D. Deyermond, J.R. Little and J.E. Varey

25.	Geoghegan, C.	Louis Aragon: essai de bibliographie.
		I. Œuvres, Tome 1 (1918-1959), 1979
		I. Œuvres, Tome 2 (1960-1977), 1979
		II. Critique, *in preparation*
26.	Lowe, D.K.	Benjamin Constant: an annotated bibliography of critical editions and studies (1946-1978), 1979
27.	Mason, B.	Michel Butor: a checklist, 1979
		Supplement No.1, *in preparation*
28.	Shirt, D.J.	The Old French Tristan poems: a bibliographical guide, 1980
29.	McGaha, M.D.	The Theatre in Madrid during the Second Republic: a checklist, 1979
30.	Stathatos, C.C.	A Gil Vicente bibliography (1940-1975), with a preface by Thomas R. Hart, 1980
		Supplement No.1, *in preparation*
31.	Bleikasten, A.	Arp: bibliographie
		I. Ecrits/Dichtung, 1981
		II. Critique/Kritik, 1983
32.	Bergman, H.E., and S. E. Szmuk,	A Catalogue of Comedias sueltas in the New York Public Library, 2 vols, I. A-H, 1980; II. I-Z, 1981
33.	Best, M.	Ramón Pérez de Ayala: an annotated bibliography of criticism, 1980
34.	Clive, H.P.	Marguerite de Navarre: an annotated bibliography, 1983
35.	Sargent-Baur, B.N., and R.F. Cook,	*Aucassin et Nicolete*: a critical bibliography, 1981
36.	Nelson, B.	Emile Zola: a selective analytical bibliography, 1982
37.	Field, T.	Maurice Barrès: a selective critical bibliography (1948-1979), 1982
38.	Bell, S.M.	Nathalie Sarraute: a bibliography, 1982
39.	Kinder, A.G.	Spanish Protestants and Reformers in the Sixteenth Century: a bibliography, 1983
40.	Clive, H.P.	Clément Marot: an annotated bibliography, 1983
41.	Whinnom, K.	The Spanish Sentimental Romance 1440-1550: a critical bibliography, 1983
42.	Kennedy, A.J.	Christine de Pizan: a bibliographical guide, 1984
43.	Tremewan, P.	Prévost: an analytical bibliography of criticism to 1981, 1984
44.	Holloway, J.B.	Brunetto Latini: an analytic bibliography, 1986
45.	Craddock, J.R.	The Legislative Works of Alfonso X, el Sabio: a critical bibliography, 1986